"This book is not only for grandparents but also for everyone who longs to crawl into the arms of God as their Abba Daddy and snuggle secure in the wonder of his love for his children."

— BETTY VELDMAN WIELAND, coauthor of
Growing People Through Small Groups

"Donna has an eye to catch glimpses of the extraordinary in the ordinary, an ear to hear wisdom in the most mundane of moments. So find a comfortable chair and take in the enchantment."

— GERALD L. SITTSER, professor of theology, Whitworth College;
author of *A Grace Disguised*

"There's deep wisdom in these brief narratives, told with charm, insight, and the gift of a natural storyteller. I was moved and blessed."

— LUCI SHAW, author of *The Genesis of It All*;
writer-in-residence, Regent College

"I encourage you to stop, take a moment, and read these priceless stories. Learn through a child's eyes what hope really is: the confident expectation that God is in the small moments of ordinary days."

— MARLAE GRITTER, executive vice president,
Moms In Touch International

"Donna's engaging work reminds us that there is so much we do not see. Through the wide-open eyes of her grandchildren, she opens our eyes to the beauty and wonder of God's world."

— ALVIN J. VANDER GRIEND, DMin, author of
Love to Pray: A 40-Day Devotional for Deepening Your Prayer Life

"As a new grandmother, I find Donna Vander Griend's stories to be captivating, encouraging, and heartwarming. She makes me look forward to the journey of discovery and faith-building with my grandchildren."

— LEONA BERGSTROM, director, Lifetime Ministry; author of
Amazing Grays: Unleashing the Power of Age in Your Congregation

Donna Vander Griend

Out of the Mouths of GRANDBABES

BEDTIME STORIES FOR GRANDPARENTS

NAVPRESS®

BRINGING TRUTH TO LIFE

OUR GUARANTEE TO YOU

We believe so strongly in the message of our books that we are making this quality guarantee to you. If for any reason you are disappointed with the content of this book, return the title page to us with your name and address and we will refund to you the list price of the book. To help us serve you better, please briefly describe why you were disappointed. Mail your refund request to: NavPress, P.O. Box 35002, Colorado Springs, CO 80935.

The Navigators is an international Christian organization. Our mission is to advance the gospel of Jesus and His kingdom into the nations through spiritual generations of laborers living and discipling among the lost. We see a vital movement of the gospel, fueled by prevailing prayer, flowing freely through relational networks and out into the nations where workers for the kingdom are next door to everywhere.

NavPress is the publishing ministry of The Navigators. The mission of NavPress is to reach, disciple, and equip people to know Christ and make Him known by publishing life-related materials that are biblically rooted and culturally relevant. Our vision is to stimulate spiritual transformation through every product we publish.

© 2007 by Donna Vander Griend

All rights reserved. No part of this publication may be reproduced in any form without written permission from NavPress, P.O. Box 35001, Colorado Springs, CO 80935.
www.navpress.com

NAVPRESS, BRINGING TRUTH TO LIFE, and the NAVPRESS logo are registered trademarks of NavPress. Absence of ® in connection with marks of NavPress or other parties does not indicate an absence of registration of those marks.

ISBN-13: 978-1-57683-858-7
ISBN-10: 1-57683-858-7

Cover design by Charles Brock, thedesignworksgroup.com
Cover illustration by Istockphoto.com
Creative Team: Terry Behimer, Liz Heaney, Cara Iverson, Kathy Mosier, Arvid Wallen, Kathy Guist

Some of the anecdotal illustrations in this book are true to life and are included with the permission of the persons involved. All other illustrations are composites of real situations, and any resemblance to people living or dead is coincidental.

Unless otherwise identified, all Scripture quotations in this publication are taken from *THE MESSAGE* (MSG). Copyright © 1993, 1994, 1995, 1996, 2000, 2001, 2002. Used by permission of NavPress Publishing Group. Other versions used include the *Revised Standard Version Bible* (RSV), copyright 1946, 1952, 1971, by the Division of Christian Education of the National Council of the Churches of Christ in the USA, used by permission, all rights reserved; the *Good News Bible Today's English Version* (TEV), copyright © American Bible Society 1966, 1971, 1976; and the *King James Version* (KJV).

Vander Griend, Donna, 1942-
  Out of the mouths of grandbabes : bedtime stories for grandparents /
Donna Vander Griend.
     p. cm.
  Includes bibliographical references.
  ISBN 1-57683-858-7
  1. Grandparents--Religious life. 2. Grandchildren--Anecdotes. I.
Title.
BV4528.5.G75 2007
242'.645--dc22
                              2006025565

Printed in the United States of America

1 2 3 4 5 6 7 8 / 11 10 09 08 07

FOR A FREE CATALOG OF NAVPRESS BOOKS & BIBLE STUDIES,
CALL 1-800-366-7788 (USA) OR 1-800-839-4769 (CANADA).

To my favorite storytellers, living messengers of God's love.

Our grandchildren:
Anthony James Robert
Samuel Keith
Caleb Joseph Francis
Jack Skyler
Emmett Michael
Josiah Kahelemeakua
Lily Kate
Malakai Kamauli'oli
Isabel Malia

Our children:
Keith and Cindy Vander Griend
Kerry and Donna-Lea Vander Griend
James and Janelle Maiocco
Kurt and Maluhia Vander Griend

CONTENTS

Foreword

"Green makes me smile." It is a green-splashed spring morning. Jack, a preschooler, speaks the words casually but reverently. His grandmother hears an echo of St. Paul's benediction in Jack's comment: "May the God of green hope fill you up with joy, fill you up with peace, so that your believing lives, filled with the life-giving energy of the Holy Spirit, will brim over with hope!" (Romans 15:13).

The grandmother, Donna Vander Griend, does this a lot—expertly discerns the scriptural allusions, the artless gospel-echoing remarks in the talk of her grandchildren (she has nine of them), and then passes them on to us in brief parable-stories. As we read her stories and listen through her attentive grandparent ears, we acquire a mindset that hears—really hears—the innocence and purity of revealed gospel truth that comes out of the mouths of babes and grandbabes. She is a conspicuous instance of grandson Jack's "God of green hope," still flourishing in his grandmother, who is "ever full of sap and green to show that the Lord is upright" (see Psalm 104:16; 92:15). Through the unstudied, spontaneous language of our grandchildren, we can eavesdrop on the whispers of the Holy Spirit in our everyday lives.

Grandparents ourselves, we have been reading these stories by Donna Vander Griend for a couple of years now. We frequently read—and reread—them to one another as bedtime stories. The kinds of stories we once read to our children are now coming back to us in the lives and language of our grandchildren. We didn't expect this. We don't know of another book like this, written out of a remarkable and surprising collaboration between grandchildren and grandparent. We treasure these stories, not only for the delight they convey and the memories they evoke but also as an extended and convincing confirmation of Isaiah's words that "a little child shall lead them" (11:6, KJV).

Eugene and Jan Peterson

Acknowledgments

To Cheryl Bostrom, who taught me to write by whacking at thistles without wounding me, sifting through chaff without diminishing me, finding the wheat and promising me it would multiply fiftyfold. These stories would not have grown without you.

To my children and their grace-chosen spouses, whose eyes opened along with mine to the holy moments their children (my grandchildren) were producing. Thank you for noticing, reporting in, and saying, "This isn't just for grandparents. Parents need to read these stories too."

To Gert and Tony DeKruyf for being the first grandparents to hear the stories read aloud. "Read us another one!" you kept saying while your daughter Lori's love of literature broadened to include this book.

To the students from Whitworth College who were in Dr. Jerry Sittser's Christian spirituality class: January interim, 2005. Thank you for begging, "Tell us a story before we go to bed." And thank you, Jerry, for allowing the deep theology of the day's lectures to end with these stories of childlike faith.

To my small groups: The Purple Sisters, the Restoration House bunch, my breakfast club at Shari's, the couples' gathering from church. Your prayers and encouragement turned the writing from dread to joy.

To my editors at NavPress for taking this publishing risk and to Liz Heaney for calling my manuscript "clean and delightful."

To Orv for making time chunks and solitary places happen so that I could write, for sharing these grandkids with me in ways only their grandfather could, and for using the phrase "best seller" in your overexpectant prayers. I love you.

To Jan Peterson, who read these stories at bedtime to Eugene with a charm and expression that motivated him to help get them published. You have both championed the ongoing stories of ordinary people (like us and our grandchildren) and made it clear that you, too, are among the ordinary. "Children are our first defense against the deadening and flattening effects of disconnecting God and life. . . . We lose the immediacy, spontaneity, and exuberance of resurrection life [without them]."[1] What grand motivation for writing about children!

To Creator God, who let me shimmy into a tiny cleft of creativity and hide there until the stories came and I knew that I, my children, and my children's children were made in his image, beloved characters all.

Introduction

We say about a really good story, "I just ate it up." As I watch our grandchildren's antics and dialogue unfold into the ingredients of story, I grow spiritually from these soul-salivating meals served up by God's hand: holy, improbable moments of delicious fare. I hear truth simplified; I experience perfect praise; I see creation anew through child-eyes; I feel God's love through a wider embrace; I sense wonder; and I trust God yet again with a childlike faith. The children in my life have fed me a banquet beyond belief that has made me a believer all over again.

God did not stop creating stories after putting the period at the end of Revelation. The Author of all stories is still writing, as involved in our third millennium as he was in the biblical accounts of the Israelites and the Passion of Christ. Someone has said that because God likes stories so much, he made people. He starts all people out little, the size of children. I suspect he casts children in his current dramas because he knows our love for them will jump-start our listening skills. Make reservations for the best seats at your grandchildren's story sessions, and come early. Your youngsters will turn the ordinary into sacramental delights for your hungry hearts.

PART ONE

SIMPLE TRUTHS

*The disciples came up and asked, "Why do you tell stories?" [Jesus] replied,
". . . To create readiness, to nudge the people toward receptive insight."*

Matthew 13:10-11,13

*All Jesus did that day was tell stories—a long storytelling afternoon. His
storytelling fulfilled the prophecy: I will open my mouth and tell stories; I will
bring out into the open things hidden since the world's first day.*

Matthew 13:34-35

1
Rules

"Treat one another justly . . . be compassionate with each other. Don't take advantage . . . don't plot and scheme against one another."

Zechariah 7:9-10

Like all children from the beginning of time, my grandchildren make up their own rules. Before they could read, they played Trivial Pursuit by completely dispensing of the need for trivia question-and-answer cards. They simply took turns throwing the dice and then moving the circle container the right number of spaces, filling it with the pie piece that matched the color they just landed on and waiting to see who had a pie-full first.

This afternoon Jack and Sam sit by our breakfast nook, negotiating rules for a game called King's Cribbage, a meshing of Scrabble with a Cribbage scoring system. The flat wooden blocks have letters and numbers on them, but instead of the whole alphabet, only the letters from the traditional pack of cards appear: J, Q, K, and A. The tiles come in two colors. The game goes far beyond what a preschooler and first grader can accomplish with their current mathematical or literary skills, so the age-appropriate rules begin to emerge:

> "How about you win if you get all the Ks by the end?" suggests one brother.
> "And they have to all be the same color, right?" chimes in the other.
> "And you're not allowed to see any of the letters."
> "Yeah, so put them on the bench under the tablecloth."

A few months ago these two turned Dominoes into a game of flight and fantasy. "Line up the ones with the most dots on them into two long rows, Grandma. Those will be the runway lights."

I cooperated by getting down on the wood floor and grabbing game pieces. "Then turn all the other ones to the black side and put them in between for the airplanes to land on. Don't leave any spaces between them, or the airplane might crash."

My grandkids have rules for outdoor games, too. For instance, if the sprinkler is on under the trampoline on a hot summer day, you have to slide on the trampoline through the water on your stomach, or roll through it, or sit on top of the water flow. But everyone has to do the same thing as everyone else, and everyone has to take turns. If the little kids are on the trampoline, the bigger kids have to jump on their knees, not on their feet.

On another afternoon, grandsons Anthony and Caleb went down to the pool table room. In place on the floor at either end of the pool table sits a red camel saddle their grandpa had purchased in Turkey during his naval assignment on the Mediterranean. Our grandchildren have stood on those two upholstered stools and rolled pool balls back and forth over the table since toddlerhood. Anthony is taller now, so he knelt on the little stool. Caleb took the traditional standing position. The brothers started making up the rules:

"If my plain ball hits your striped ball, I get a point," said one.

"No, how about we get as many points as the number on the ball?"

"That's not fair! My white ball doesn't have any number on it!"

"Well, let's set up with this thing," Anthony said as he placed the triangular ball rack on the pool table and put his balls in the middle of it.

"No," countered Caleb as he lined up his balls into groups of twos and threes, staggering them like battalions on a battlefield. "I'm doing mine this way."

They began rolling their balls toward their opponent, creating what looked like chaos to me but seemed to make perfect sense to them. The balls cracked together, landed in the pockets, were retrieved, and went on another roll. Though I could not figure out why, Caleb was falling behind.

Anthony, observing that his little brother's stance on the stool put him too high to eyeball his targets and aim well, offered some big-brother advice: "You need to kneel, Caleb. Life goes better that way."

There it is. The number one rule in this game called life: Pray!

We fall on our knees before you, Father. We pray for the power and discipline to obey you—and when we do not, we ask for the humble acceptance of your forgiveness and grace. Amen.

2

SOUP AND SPROUTS

The river itself, on both banks, will grow fruit trees of all kinds. Their leaves won't wither, the fruit won't fail. Every month they'll bear fresh fruit because the river from the Sanctuary flows to them. Their fruit will be for food and their leaves for healing.

Ezekiel 47:12

This afternoon our grandson came to visit us after preschool and wanted to draw at our kitchen table. "I need felt pens and stickers, Grandma," Jack asked. Then he started to work and play on cream-colored construction paper, scrawling watery, wavy blue lines across the bottom of the page.

I peeled carrots and made soup, silently observing from the sidelines. When he finished his drawing, I asked him to tell me about it. "There's no story, Grandma. Only a picture."

But then he began pointing out the particulars in his picture, from the top on down. "These are falling dragons shooting out sparks and fire. The green dragon's horns are falling off because he struck the tree so hard that a branch fell into the river."

"What are these little red balls, Jack?"

"Those are from the apple tree that the dragon broke. The apples are still falling." He paused then, wanting my full attention. "And see this dot that I made with my pencil? That's a seed that fell out of one of the apples. It's next to the river and it's going to grow a new tree. And see this stump? It's already started growing."

Unknowingly, Jack has pointed me to parts of Revelation and Ezekiel as well as Isaiah:

> "The country will look like pine and oak forest
> with every tree cut down—

Every tree a stump, a huge field of stumps.
   But there's a holy seed in those stumps."
   (Isaiah 6:13)

A green Shoot will sprout from Jesse's stump,
   from his roots a budding Branch.
The life-giving Spirit of GOD will hover over him,
   the Spirit that brings wisdom and understanding.
   (Isaiah 11:1-2)

   This small prophet has never heard about the metaphors of a life-giving river, spiritual warfare, a holy seed, a budding branch, or a shooting sprout. He doesn't know how those biblical pictures predict and tell the story of Jesus. Yet he draws, drawing on some creative mystery within the sanctuary of his five-year-old being. As he explained his simple truths to me, his grandmother, I believed all over again with the faith of a child.

Thank you, God, for inspiring children to draw pictures, for moving little hands across a page, finger-scrunching a pen, shaping stumps and seeds, green sprouts and deep blue rivers. Thank you that your Word is full of pictures, too, and that your prophecies come true. Amen.

3

WAITING

There's . . . a right time for everything on the earth:
A right time for birth and another for death . . .
A right time to lament and another to cheer . . .
A right time to hold on and another to let go.

Ecclesiastes 3:1-2,4,6

A baby boy, Malakai, was born just days ago to our youngest son and his wife. Their final weeks of waiting, punctuated by false-alarm trips to the hospital, are over at last. Our eighth grandchild came into the world just before midnight, timed, we trust, as God planned.

His grandfather and I are ecstatic about another healthy grandson. When we find our voices, we shout, "Yes!" to God. But soon we choke with grief again over those not with us. Malia, Malakai's maternal grandmother, died before she could greet him. We've endured this before. A few months earlier, our baby granddaughter, Lily Kate, was born just before my dad, her great-grandfather, died of a long fight to simply breathe. He held her, but that was all.

When my dad died, my mother wanted it to be her time too. Face taut and fists tight, she spoke out of deep frustration and grief, "I'll probably live forty years yet." But when her great-grandson Malakai was born, she covered her hurting heart with a light and open hand, smiled, and said, "That's wonderful!"

We don't spend long in grandparent status without being shaken by the birth and death of life, the opposites that are so unlike each other we cannot believe the same God invented both. With alarm I often wonder how we hold the extreme feelings of joy and grief simultaneously within our spirits without imploding.

Baby Malakai's cousins and their parents and Orv and I went to the hospital to meet him. We all took turns carrying the newborn and hugging each other. When our oldest grandson (age eight) held our youngest grandson in his arms, I asked him what he thought about the passage of time, since that was what was on my mind. "Sometimes it goes fast, and sometimes it goes slow, Grandma."

"When does it go the most slowly for you, Anthony?"

"When I'm bored," he answered quickly.

"And what's the most boring thing you do?"

"Wait."

We waited for Malakai to be born. My mother waits for life's end.

At nearly eight times Anthony's age, I am not bored, nor does time go slowly, but I am also waiting for something. I am restless, not knowing how to rejoice well without sorrowing and sorrow too much without rejoicing. Time slipping by saddens me. I wait; time doesn't. Author Gina Bria writes that we have "a spiritual problem—the immortal soul cinched in an hourglass."[2] It hurts.

The psalmist says, "I pray to God—my life a prayer—and wait for what he'll say and do." (130:5). One day that same God will break the hourglass and set us free!

Timeless God, thank you for births and deaths and the living in between. Forgive us for wasting time and also for wanting to hold on to it so desperately. Grant us your peace as we wait. Amen.

4
REMODELING

You get us ready for life: you probe for our soft spots,
you knock off our rough edges.
And I'm feeling so fit, so safe: made right, kept right.
God in solemn honor does things right, but his nerves
are sandpapered raw.

Psalm 7:10-11

Our son Keith is remodeling the last corner of his house: the utility room and bathroom. After hours of hammering, caulking, plastering, painting, and sanding, he and Kerry, his brother, have redeemed the spaces in this rambling shack enough to make them qualify for a *House Beautiful* magazine cover. Their best strategy for redemption, though, is to install skylights and let the light break through the Pacific Northwest dreariness of rain clouds and the shadows of towering evergreens.

With one skylight to go, Keith sets a ladder in place next to the carport and climbs to the roof corner above the utility room. He makes a hole in his roof, and as the noise and dust mingle, his little boys become curious and (with their mother's help) climb the ladder to the flat carport roof. Their dad lays down the rules: "Sam and Jack, see that stack of two-by-fours? Stay on this side of it. And see those bundles of shingles? They are your fence on that side."

I climb the ladder to check progress once the skylight installation is well under way. My grandsons, surprised to see their grandma's head rise above the roofline and heady with the heights they have also climbed, dance and shout together on the rooftop.

The boys stay on the roof for a long time. Mid-afternoon they have a request: "Dad, can we use this stuff to build something?"

He nods permission. They banter high-level engineering instructions back and forth:

"Move this board over there, okay?"

"How 'bout putting two of these on top of each other to make the cars go faster?"

They move and adjust the scattered lumber, choosing two-by-fours for straightaways and slanted shingles as off-ramps, imagining future travels for their Matchbox cars.

The skyway complete, they make their way down the ladder, their father giving guidance from above as they work at foot placement and balance and handholds: "Wait 'til your foot feels the rung, then bring your other foot down." "Leave some space for Jack, Sam. Don't step on his fingers." "Careful, now . . . slowly . . . " When the boys reach firm ground, they run to the toy box, where they each choose two of their favorite race cars.

Even though Keith cannot see his sons over the pitch of the roof, he hears them return to the bottom of the ladder. "Okay, guys. Make sure you hold on tight. Put one hand on each side of the ladder, and don't let go, no matter what."

Jack looks down at his car-filled hands. Forgetting that he has pockets in his jeans, he stuffs both cars in his mouth, clamping his teeth over their front hoods and wheels. He begins his steady climb, obeying his father's counsel as his freed hands now shimmy tightly up the ladder's aluminum sides. As he rises to the top, he sees his dad bent over his work and wants to announce with some pride what a good son he has been: following orders exactly and achieving his goal besides. "Dad . . ." Out tumble the cars; they clank down the ladder. Jack's downcast eyes catch the cars' final clunk on the driveway below; his ears catch his dad's laughter. A second separates tragedy and comedy. Jack chooses laughter and lets his sides split.

Next time I come to visit, I must remember to tell Jack about Aesop's fable "The Fox and the Crow."

The fox wanted the cheese in the crow's beak and deceitfully flattered her to get it. "Good-day, Mistress Crow," he cried.

"How well you are looking today: how glossy your feathers; how bright your eye. I feel sure your voice must surpass that of other birds, just as your figure does; let me hear but one song from you that I may greet you as the Queen of Birds." The crow lifted up her head and began to caw her best, but the moment she opened her mouth the piece of cheese fell to the ground, only to be snapped up by the fox. [3]

Jack, humbled but whole, will most certainly laugh again.

Dear God, thank you for humor that descends like a dove, for laughter that erupts from a father, and for sons set free to chuckle at a mistake. How human to err, even in the midst of obedience. Thank you for the sacrifice of your suffering that makes us safe, freeing us to laugh and dance on the rooftops of our lives. Amen.

5

NEIGHBORS

*Jesus said, "'Love the Lord your God with all your passion
and prayer and intelligence.'
This is the most important, the first on any list. But there is
a second to set alongside it:
'Love others as well as you love yourself.'"*

Matthew 22:37-39

"Mom, there are shoes hanging from the wire over our front side-walk," Anthony announces, not knowing whether this is urgent or funny. His mom and I go to the front window to take in this change of sight. Swaying from a telephone wire that stretches from a utility pole to the house is a large pair of black tennis shoes. The shoestrings had been tied end-to-end before the shoes were flung skyward so that the strings looped over the wire and stayed there, weighted down by two size-twelves.

My brother-in-law Jim, a utility lineman, tells me that this has happened often in the last few years. It is a fad, he says, for high school seniors to put their signatures on each other's well-worn shoes and then toss them over telephone wires to stand as a milestone marking their graduation.[4]

Anthony's dad and grandpa brainstorm how to remove the shoes; one solution includes going to Handy-Andy Rental down the street and procuring a ten-foot extension gizmo with a nonconductive han-dle. We watch from the window as father and grandfather maneuver the long-handled tool around the moving tennis shoes. It makes me smile to see a lawyer and his father-in-law surgeon working together, one getting the rubber pincers in place while the other waits for the right moment to pull the long cord attached to the handles that will make the grabbers close around a shoe's cuff or toe. Faces tipped skyward, the men sway, the tool circles, and the shoes dance. The lawyer aims; the doctor pulls. Finally, the pair of shoes plops to the ground. Son-in-law James picks them up and delivers them to the woman across the street. Her teenage son is angry. He cusses loudly, jumps into his pickup, starts the motor, and then accelerates madly, tires squealing down the city street.

Anthony is perched on the arm of the couch in the living room, clearly bothered by what he has just seen. His sensitivity creates a furrow between his eyebrows. He looks down at his grandma lounging on the couch and deems her a listener. "Maybe I'm too glad about this," he confesses. "What I'm glad about is that I don't have to look at those ugly tennis shoes the rest of my life." Torn between loving himself more than he loves his neighbor, he adds, "I feel bad for that teenager, though."

Later that evening, his father debriefs him about the incident, explaining that throwing shoes over telephone wires is not acceptable. "I guess teenagers lose their minds sometimes," Anthony reflects.

In five years Anthony will be a teenager. I hope he has a sympathetic neighbor.

Our Father God, we want very much to obey your commands. Teach us how to love you and our neighbors well, with a passion that cares, prayers that appeal for your help, and solutions that are intelligent. Amen.

6

DR. SEUSS

Generous in love — God, give grace!
Huge in mercy — wipe out my bad record.
Scrub away my guilt, soak out my sins in your laundry . . .
scrub me and I'll have a snow-white life.

Psalm 51:1-2,7

Book collector Josiah specializes in Dr. Seuss. He looks for the Cat in the Hat logo on the corner of each book's cover and then gathers, stacks, and carries his special Seuss pile to his daily destinations: the couch, the toy room floor, his grandparents' house, the kitchen table (to keep them out of baby brother's reach). In his honor, all of Josiah's third birthday presents were by Dr. Seuss.

He requests readings often. He peels each tome off the pile, announcing its title: "*ABC*, by Dr. Seuss. Read this one, Grandma."

"Here, Grandpa," he says as he works through the pile and reads another title.

"*There's a Wocket in My Pocket*, by Dr. Seuss."

"Now this one: *Hop on Pop*, by Dr. Seuss." As we turn the pages, he recites the lilting rhythms, taking memory cues from the cartoon illustrations.

During a naptime talk-to-himself session, Josiah repeats his litany of titles. His father overhears him add a concluding title, "*Josiah*, by Dr. Seuss." Grinning, his dad pokes his head through the bedroom door and corrects his offspring: "No, Josiah. It's *Josiah*, by Mommy and Daddy."

"*Josiah by Mommy and Daddy*, by Dr. Seuss," Josiah self-corrects.

He finds lyrical titles in everyday dialogue. "It's a great day,

Grandma," I hear him say.

"Why is it a great day, Josiah?" I ask.

"The leaves," he says.

"Green and yellow ones," I say to add color.

"*Green Leaves and Yellow*, by Dr. Seuss," he lilts. *Green Eggs and Ham*, I think to myself.

Later Josiah looks at the natural-wood toilet seat when we go into the bathroom. "A donut," he says. We lift it up and notice the oblong rubber buffers on its backside. "Hot dogs," he names them. "*Donuts and Hot Dogs*, by Dr. Seuss." Yet another title finds its way into his repertoire.

We adults catch this singsong contagion for titles. A friend dines with us during an election campaign; she bemoans the difficulties of trying to filter out political spin from truth and of piecing together the liberal and conservative views. "I'm confused but balanced," she says and then laughs. "*Confused but Balanced*, by Dr. Seuss," we hear ourselves respond.

Josiah sits next to us with his slightly worn favorite: *ABC*, by Dr. Seuss. He opens the first page. Head bobbing and sounding like a rap artist, he quotes the lines: "Big A little a, What [beniggus] with A? Aunt Annie's alligator . . . . A . . a . . A."[5]

He jumps from the bench and opens the quick-reach drawer that holds my leftover household gadgets ready for child play: an aluminum egg separator that clangs, wooden spoons that clap, tea strainers that open and close, a ketchup dispenser to squeeze, and plastic bibs for catchalls. Josiah picks out a bent-bristled, red toothbrush from the bottom of the drawer and goes back to his book. He proceeds to scrub the big 'A' and the little 'a' and Seuss's Aunt Annie and her alligator with the toothbrush. He turns the page and scrubs the B letters along with the barber and baby and bumblebee. "Big F little f, F . . f . . F," he raps and then does his toothbrush rubbing all over the "Four fluffy feathers on a Fiffer-feffer-feff."[6]

"What are you doing, Josiah?" I ask.

"I cleaning the ABC's, Grandma," he answers.

He turns two pages at a time and notices that he has missed

the D. He lovingly backs up and gives the donuts and the duck-dog a thorough scrubbing. He doesn't miss a single letter. I like his concept: cleaning letters before they go into words. Perhaps words of truth and sanctified imagination would have a better chance if they could reach the printed page unblemished.

Josiah is on the last page when Grandpa walks into the room, eyes the book-and-brush exercise, and asks, "What are you doing, Josiah?"

"I cleaning 'Zizzer-Zazzer-Zuzz as you can plainly see,'"[7] Josiah quotes as he closes the book on the last less-than-beautiful, fuzzy-checkered Seuss character. I like this concept of cleaning imperfect characters too — characters with warts and bumps and shriveled Grinch-hearts that are too small. Forgiveness scrubbing done out of love. Big G little g, What beniggus with G? Guilt and gone and generous grace . . . G . . g . . G.

God of mercy, thank you for figuring out how to do away with our guilt. Continue to soak and scrub us in your mercy and grace. Write us into your Book of Life so that we can share every perfectly clean letter, word, and page of eternity with you. Amen.

7

GEMS AND SPIDERS

Love from the center of who you are; don't fake it. Run for dear life from evil;
hold on for dear life to good. Be good friends who love deeply. . . . Discover
beauty in everyone.

Romans 12:9-10,17

One rainy afternoon, seven-year-old Sam persuaded me to boot up my laptop. We waited together as the screen lit up and the icons appeared. He challenged me to find a computer game, giving advice all the while on clicks and arrows and mouse movements, grandson mentoring grandmother. Together we succeeded.

We found a game called Gem Hunt, in which the player tries to find hidden jewels within the walls and garden of a castle without running into spiders. Each time Sam uncovered a gem, a crystal prism showed up mid-screen. Then a paintbrush floated across the screen to color it in: red for rubies, purple for amethysts, green for emeralds. Fully graced with color, each gem dropped with a tinkling sound into a treasure box. Whenever a can with a spider label showed up on the screen, Sam would press delete to wipe out each scary threat from the tarantula squad. As he eyed the scorekeeping square, Sam was sure he was winning: twenty gems, zero spiders. "Game over!" the computer announced in robot-ese, which translated means, "Sam, you lose." He groaned and slumped.

Sam could not believe he had lost the game. We tried to figure out why. We backtracked and realized that we had failed to read the instructions, which told us that the spiders Sam was destroying stood for *cans of spider spray*, not the spiders themselves. He had been deleting spray cans when he thought he was killing spiders. He needed a supply of that protective spider spray if he was to continue adding to his gem collection without the spiders stopping him. He got it. "No spray, no play," he announced as he pressed "Start" for another game.

When we finally shut down the computer, Sam got talkative, a relief after his mesmerized silence. "We should have read the instructions, that's for sure," he said, breaking out of computer mode and into live conversation. His reflection continued, "You know, Grandma, that game was like hunting for good friends. Gotta find gems, not spiders that are bad to you." His words reminded me of a C. S. Lewis quote from *The Four Loves*:

> Friendship . . . is the instrument by which God reveals to each the beauties of all the others. . . . In each of my friends there is something that only some other friend can fully bring out . . . other lights than my own to show all the facets.[8]

"Gotta find gems for friends." Press "Enter."
Sam, my friend, you win.

God of relationships, thank you for choosing us for one another. Help us reflect back the beauties of each person you bring into our lives, without the impurities of envy or comparison, so that we see each other deeply dazzled in your love. Amen.

PART TWO

PERFECT PRAISE

"Out of the mouth of babes . . . thou hast brought perfect praise."
Matthew 21:16, RSV

8

OF CROWNS AND KINGS

The next day the huge crowd that had arrived for the Feast heard that Jesus was entering Jerusalem. They broke off palm branches and went out to meet him. And they cheered: Hosanna! Blessed is he who comes in God's name! Yes! The King of Israel!

John 12:12-13

Architecturally speaking, every home that houses children should have a parade route—a circular traffic pattern of doors and arches that open through walls—for unending chases, motoring, and marching. Our home effectively handles a donkey-gray desk chair on wheels. Two children can ride it, while another pushes. The child-loaded chair lurches and spins from foyer to living room, rolls left through the dining room into the kitchen, takes another left through the den area, and circles back to the tiled foyer. Carpet and rugs slow the chair down after fast track tiles; high decibel boy-noise adds fuel.

Once, when the cranky Pharisees were complaining to Jesus about children running through the temple and shouting, "Hosanna to David's Son!" Jesus responded by paraphrasing Psalm 8:2: "Out of the mouth of babes . . . thou hast brought perfect praise" (Matthew 21:16, RSV). We grandparents try to listen for hosannas through the din. We try to remember that Jesus chose to enter into the loop of our lives through surprising ways: mangers and crosses and riding on donkeys in Palm Sunday parades.

It is our eldest son and wife's turn to welcome us all into their home for dinner. I notice for the first time that their indoor blueprint doesn't include "the children's circle." Six stay-put grandchildren litter the costume contents of an old ship's trunk over the living room floor, bargain and negotiate for wardrobe remnants and accessories, try on identities and then change them again. One becomes a knight with plastic breastplate and lightweight sword; another a pirate with an eye patch and a three-cornered hat. Still another strips down to his cartooned skivvies and dons cowboy boots, a belt, and a Stetson hat. They capture the adults (willing hostages) to form an audience for their dramas, in which they make entrances and exits from behind the sofa.

Toddler Josiah, whose name reminds me of the boy king of Israel, asks his mother to help him get his Uncle Keith's white T-shirt over his head. It swaddles him in a flowing, floor-length robe. From the antique trunk he grabs a shiny, plastic crown, complete with jeweled baubles and regal points, and places it on his head. The other children take one look at him and, en masse, start a parade route, running down the hallway, through the bedroom, out the back door, over the lawn and outside deck, back into the house again, and through double doors into the living room, all the while shouting, "Here comes the king! The king is coming!"

Josiah gives chase, following the newly mapped traffic circle. He trips on the T-shirt; his crown drops over one eye and rests on his nose. He falls further behind.

Soon, though, the older cousins come up behind him, having lapped him on the circle. They domino-bump to a noisy halt and then begin marching in step behind him. Josiah leads the parade, laughing at their presence and their submission. Turning his head now and then to make sure of his following, he moves triumphantly through hallways and doors.

A toddler becomes king.

King Jesus, we are baffled by the incarnation. How did the ruler of the universe become a baby? And the baby become king again? Forgive us for misunderstanding what your kingship and your kingdom are all about. Thank you for entering into the cycle of human life to save us. Help us follow your marching orders willingly and well. Amen.

9

LIGHTBULBS

"If I make you light-bearers, you don't think I'm going to hide you under a bucket, do you? I'm putting you . . . on a light stand—shine! Keep open house; be generous with your lives. By opening up to others, you'll prompt people to open up with God."

Matthew 5:15-16

Bedtime. Trading his comfortable recliner for Jack and Sam's bedroom floor, Keith leans against the side of the bed for a backrest. His little boys, pajama-ed and eager, tummy-wriggle over the quilt on the bottom bunk, position their heads on either side of his to be level-headed with Dad, and hand-cup their jaws at an angle to best see the pictures.

Tonight's first selection from the book pile is *Weslandia*. Keith always reads the cover to his children: title, author, and illustrator. Sometimes he even selects a sentence from the book flap as a good starter sentence: "This fantastical picture book, like its hero, is bursting at the seams with creativity." Then he opens the book.

One of the first illustrations shows ten-year-old Wesley, eyes bright with lightning zigzags shooting ideas into his airspace through thick eyeglasses. The text reads, "Suddenly, Wesley's thoughts shot sparks. His eyes blazed."[9] Wesley does not fit into his town of cloned houses and cars and boys with the same haircuts. Resisting this sameness, he invents his own civilization, Weslandia, which has new ways to tell time, score games, make mosquito repellent, name stars, write with an eighty-letter alphabet, and concoct recipes.

When the story is finished, Jack turns to his Dad and asks, "Why do people want to be all the same?"

"Because it's easier that way," Keith replies. "It's like having a lightbulb in your head. If you never think, the lightbulb goes off. Then you just do the same things as everyone else."

"I think my lightbulb goes off when I always order the same thing at McDonald's," Jack says. "Maybe it's halfway on when I eat different things sometimes."

"When is my lightbulb off, Dad?" asks Sam.

"Well, probably when you watch too much TV or play too many video games. There's no chance then for your mind to have its own idea—for your lightbulb to go on."

Later in the week when Jack and Sam come to our home for a morning, they ask to watch television. "Okay," I relent, "but not for very long. I don't want the lightbulbs going out in your heads." We find an animated children's program on channel five. During the first commercial, when the program is a mere ten minutes into its half hour, Sam says, "Grandma, I think we better quit watching now. I don't want my lightbulb to go off."

I gladly press the power button on the remote.

In the quiet, Jack sparkles with a new thought: "I just love babies."

"Why, Jack?" I ask.

"Because their lightbulbs are always on!"

Lord of Light, as your light-bearers, clearly and creatively made in your image, we thank you. We carry your energy within us. Help us to shine so that others will be generously blessed, opening themselves up to your light. Amen.

10
THE ABACUS

[Jesus] directed his disciples, "Sit them down in groups of about fifty."... He took the five loaves and two fish, lifted his face to heaven in prayer, blessed, broke, and gave.... After the people had all eaten their fill, twelve baskets of leftovers were gathered up.

Luke 9:14-17

In one corner of the toy room, on the highest shelf, leans the abacus. As Anthony stands in the middle of the room and considers his options for more advanced play, he spots the old Chinese hand calculator.

Anthony is ready for it, he tells me. "I'm taller now, Grandma. And I can count by tens." The abacus has rows of large movable beads that ride across thick wires. Red, blue, yellow, green, tan — two rows of each. This instrument has had a long life among us. Even as toddlers, Anthony and his cousins shoved its wooden balls back and forth, listening to them rattle, watching the bright colors slide.

He climbs on a chair and removes the abacus from its perch. His fingers move and click the beads once again. He looks around for what he can count. This is a loner activity. Just right — Anthony loves working alone. He proceeds quietly, unobserved.

Later he reports to his mother, who reports to his grandmother, "There are one thousand and eighteen people in the pictures on your walls."

"That can't be," I say in disbelief. "Anthony must have counted wrong. Are you sure he didn't mean one *hundred* and eighteen?"

"I'm sure," his mother claims. "He says it's okay if we round it off to a thousand and twenty if that's easier to remember."

I picture our grandson standing before our family portraits in the living room and then moving to our children's graduation pictures downstairs, our group pictures at weddings and Christmases lining hallways, our grandchildren's smiling faces on the dresser, all the while bracing the abacus against his abdomen with one hand, the fingers of the other hand carefully moving one colored bead after another for each aunt or uncle, mom or dad, grandpa or grandma, cousin or sibling. He knows them all, loves each face. Many of them are in more than one picture, of course. But the abacus does not discriminate. Soon Anthony is moving down the tabulating rows to the yellow tens, the red hundreds, and then even to the blue thousands.

I start to retrace his meandering path through our home. They *are* everywhere: portraits in the foyer, the bedrooms, the stairwells, even the bathrooms. I start to chuckle, then move very quickly to outright rejoicing, because one small boy started counting. No need for fingers or calculators to count one grandpa and one grandma — or five loaves and two fish, for that matter.

But when God multiplies, it's time to reach for the abacus.

Lord of millions and of me, thank you that as you look at our faces in your Book of Life, you delight in us. You do not count our sins against us but rather count each one righteous. Thank you that you subtract our sins with your sacrifice and multiply our blessings with your outstretched hand. Amen.

11

CHRISTMAS

*(What pleasure [God] took in planning this!) He wanted us to enter into the
celebration of his lavish gift-giving by
the hand of his beloved Son.*

Ephesians 1:6

We take pictures, of course. Lining up eight young grandchildren
for a portrait is like asking eels to come ashore and make a line in
the sand. One of them pouts rebelliously; three of them have stretch
marks from fake smiles. Printed, the photos record baby Lily escaping
from a bigger cousin's lap and charging in a blur that blocks out two
of the other grandchildren. Half of the grandkids have white, hollow
eyes from poor lighting; the other half have red ones. They look like
alien elves from a bad movie. No angelic icons, these. Our Christmas
album legacy is chaos and imperfection with a little hypocrisy thrown
in for denial's sake.

However, there are redemptive moments in our holiday season
that the camera does not record. Four-year-old Emmett watches as
Grandpa puts up an empty tree in our tiled foyer. "Where are the ornaments?" he asks me. "Sam and Jack can help."

"I'll find the Christmas boxes for you. Be patient. It will take me
a few minutes," I say.

As I retrieve the decorations from attic storage, I picture break-
able glass ornaments sliding from the hands of small grandsons
onto the glazed ceramic floor. I decide the adventure is worth the
risk. Emmett hops between box and tree; Jack studies each bulb; Sam
worries about balance and placement. Gladness fills the foyer as the
tree's lower limbs take on shiny gifts from little boys' hands. We break
only three.

"Where's the star?" shouts Emmett as they near the finish, remembering his own little family's traditional symbol for the tree's top. I confess that we don't have one. "Open this box, Emmett," I suggest. He finds a delicate, large, three-dimensional cross fashioned out of translucent alabaster shell and gold filigree.

"It's beautiful," he murmurs.

"Since Christmas is all about Jesus, Emmett, is it all right if we put the cross at the top of the tree?" He nods approval. Star, tree, and cross—easy icons for the eyes of a child's faith. As is the manger scene.

Our family's crèche lives on a large round coffee table for the month before Christmas. Crocheted long ago and stuffed with unbreakable cotton for our own young children, the figures continue to play their roles in several grandchild-improvised dramas as little hands hold and cuddle the baby Jesus, mix and move the Magi and shepherds, and fly the angels into living room choir stalls. On the family night designated for the retelling of the Christmas story, we hand each grandchild a character from the crèche and ask him to tell the part of the age-old story that goes with the person or animal he is holding.

Caleb holds one of the wise men and brushes up on his script before we start. "What else did they bring with the gold again?" he asks. Cues come quickly from all the generations: "Frankincense and myrrh," several voices chime. Caleb is ready.

Older brother Anthony holds Joseph. "Joseph. He had a dream," Anthony starts. "God told him to bring him and Mary into the town of Bethlehem." He places Joseph next to the manger. Cousin Sam explains that Mary becomes the mother of Jesus; he seats her next to Joseph.

Three-year-old Josiah clutches a lamb. "Would you like to put that by the manger?" I ask him.

"No, I want to keep it," he replies.

Emmett waits with his brown-yarned shepherd. When it is his turn, he looks to his dad, who says, "The angels came."

"The angels came," Emmett repeats.

"The shepherds heard a multitude in the heavens," his dad

continues. Emmett says this line about the shepherds as he holds his up for all of us to see.

"The angels were singing, 'Glory to God in the highest. Peace on earth and good will to men.'" Emmett repeats each word of his father's, each nuance, his eyes looking astonished as if seeing the story for the first time through the eyes of his shepherd.

Finally, kindergartner Jack stands up, chewing his gum and holding the baby Jesus. He walks slowly toward the nearly completed crèche and says, "Baby Jesus came to earth to die on the cross." He carefully places the embroidered bundle on the straw.

We are all quiet. Our grandkids have just brought the fragments of their childlike faith to our coffee table altar and pieced them together to form the greatest story ever told.

For the ears of a child's faith there are the Christmas carols. For as long as I can remember, six-year-old Jack has claimed "Hark! the Herald Angels Sing" as his personal favorite. When he was three and doing a rendition of the carol for the umpteenth time with the same gusto most little boys use on "Jingle Bells," I stopped him after the line "Peace on earth and mercy mild, God and sinners reconciled."[10]

"What do you think *reconciled* means, Jack?"

"It's about wrecks," he explained, picking up on the first syllable.

"Then what does *ciled* mean?" I asked, not wanting half a definition.

"To fix things."

"And who fixes all the wrecks and messes, Jack?" I asked, wondering how much more of the carol he understood.

"God does," he said and then belted out the beginning line once again, with renewed fervor: "Hark! the herald angels sing, Glory to the newborn King!"

Glory to you, God, for taking pleasure in planning the biggest celebration of all time and eternity. Thank you for inviting us to the party year after year after year. And thank you for making the invitation list multigenerational. Amen.

12

GIFTS

Can you imagine the breathtaking recovery life makes, sovereign life, in those who grasp with both hands this wildly extravagant life-gift, this grand setting-everything-right, that the one man Jesus Christ provides?

Romans 5:17

We now have eight grandchildren to buy presents for. The task overwhelms us. We fear setting nonretractable precedents for monetary amounts or sizes of packages. We worry about our reputation with the grandchildren if our choices are usually books or clothing.

We consult with the parents in our desperation. They are marginally helpful. Some think their children will be badly influenced by plastic toys as opposed to wooden ones; some are concerned about videos or monster figures that may cause nightmares; others don't want anything that shoots. Above all, we surmise, we should not bring a wrapped present into anyone's home that makes grating, repetitive noises, even if it is wrapped in a lovely bow.

Throughout this buying and giving we are torn between the theology of giving and the lure of materialism. *How can we bless rather than spoil?*

The September birthdays are coming. Lily Kate celebrates her first birthday on September third. Anthony, our eldest grandson, will be nine years old on the fourteenth. We check our schedules for a Sunday afternoon that works for everyone for the big celebration.

I go gift shopping. I want to buy the world for our only granddaughter but settle instead on a lovely hand-painted wooden pull toy: a kitten with shoulder and hip joints that sway rhythmically when a toddler drags it along by a thick, colorful strap. Lily has just learned to walk. Perfect. A doll dressed in pink also tempts me. Will her parents approve, or should the doll be more politically correct: a boy doll dressed in anything but blue? The doll's eyes close and open. Lily will be fascinated. I make the purchase.

I overhear Anthony explaining a Lego toy from his wish list to his Uncle Kurt. Later I ask Kurt for detailed information on Anthony's request and then audaciously propose that he dream up another gift idea because I want to pursue this one. He agrees. I go online to www.legoland.com, a new Internet experience for me, and try to find the toy. "It's a transformer," Anthony had said, "that turns from a helicopter into an ice sled." His hands moved while he talked, imitating the motions of putting together and taking apart.

Many a catalog picture turns up on my computer. I move from search engine to search engine, website to website. I become a frustrated novice, fearing that if I ever found what I was looking for, I would not have the courage to give out my credit card number. I confirm my membership in a generation that doesn't understand virtual reality, that needs to see a hard copy, and that is more comfortable taking a toy off a store shelf and holding it than dropping it into some virtual cart.

Surprisingly, Blue Eagle versus Snow Crawler shows up onscreen. It fits Anthony's description and matches my price range. I clinch the deal with a few clicks of the mouse. The information on the screen tells me the package will not arrive on my doorstep in time for Anthony's birthday. Too late to retract my order.

At an opportune moment, sitting at the dining room table facing my grandson, I open the conversation: "I ordered your birthday present online, Anthony, but I don't think it's going to make it on time for your birthday party. Will it be okay if you don't get your present until later?"

Anthony looks at me, his dark eyes full of meaning. Talking slowly, for impact, he says, "If you never gave me any present at all, you would still be my grandma."

In one final sentence, my nearly-nine-year-old grandson gives me the best gift of all: a love relationship.

Our Father, you who know how to give good gifts to your children, we thank you for our grandchildren. You give us moments of unconditional love from these little ones that help us receive infinities of unconditional love from you. What gifts! Amen.

13

THE TOY ROOM

Oh yes — God takes pleasure in your *pleasure!*
Dress festively every morning.
Don't skimp on colors and scarves. . . .
Make the most of each [day]!
Whatever turns up, grab it and do it. And heartily!

Ecclesiastes 9:7-10

The room that we used to call our study is now dubbed "the toy room." The name change works because, in some ways, we do less studying and more playing now anyway. The room is furnished with shelves and toy boxes that house countless objects invented solely for the purpose of keeping children busy working at playing. We have busy grandchildren.

"Let's go down to the toy room," we say to distract the baby who is threatening to cry because her parents are leaving for a night out. It usually works, for the little one knows that the lower shelves are laden with colorful playthings that tease and tantalize. She can pet soft birdies that chirp and can grip very large Legos in her chubby hands, in spite of undeveloped motor skills. A stuffed Pooh Bear and a Tigger from the bottom shelf hold her attention while one of us searches for Eeyore and Piglet to complete the cast.

The toddlers can pull the board books off the second shelf, turn their thick pages, and begin saying simple words to go with the pictures: ducky, cow, boat, ball. Grandma is there to repeat the words and reread the stories. Their thumbs and forefingers reach for the red knobs on wooden puzzle pieces as they try to fit them into their matching indentations. Grandpa guides their hands.

Hand-me-down toys left over from our children's childhoods

await our older grandkids: an Erector Set; Tinkertoys; wooden blocks (colored alphabet cubes, cylinders, and arches); Fisher Price Little People and their buildings (house, school, and hospital); Matchbox cars; a Cabbage Patch Kid named Charlie; and dress-up clothes that conjure up fads from the sixties and seventies (polyester plaids, filmy scarves, wide belts and ties).

Our grandchildren's action dramas and construction sites change over the years. The three-year-old puts the Fisher Price Little People to bed in tidy rows; the seven-year-old uses them to storm nations and take over the universe. Our toddler builds one lone block tower that keeps tipping over; our six-year-old constructs cities and underground tunnels, bridges, and laser communication centers that last until the next time he comes to play.

Taller grandchildren can reach the upper shelves in the toy room. The entertainment stored there requires even more maturity: chapter books with enchanting plots and detailed illustrations, Legos that demand dexterity and involve step-by-step instructions, and intricate marble mazes that require a basic understanding of physics. Chess and Monopoly are up there. So is the abacus.

Growing up and reaching higher: the work and play of children.

I imagine God saying to the rest of us, "Get thee to the toy room."

Dear God, thank you for your patience and pleasure in our growing process. Help us to heartily make the most of each day as we develop our spiritual skills, strengthen our outreach, accept your challenges, and imagine your purposes. Amen.

14

PENTECOST

*When the Feast of Pentecost came, they were all together
in one place. . . .
Then, like a wildfire, the Holy Spirit spread through
their ranks.*

Acts 2:1,3

Pentecost often lands on my birthday. The first promises immortality; the second effuses mortality. My misty spirit jokes with my gray matter: *Good thing my children and grandchildren are coming for the cake-and-candle deal while I can still remember their names and that they have, indeed, been here.* Some will come from three minutes down the road; others will travel the freeway from a hundred miles out.

On my Sunday-morning birthday, we join the out-of-towners to go to the church that our eldest son's family attends. Four grandsons opt to sit together, popping over each other like beanbags in a juggling act until they settle, moving arms and jumping legs finally aligned in the pew. They unfold children's bulletins and begin drawing and behaving. We look down our row at four small heads bent over their "church work." Awash in gratitude, we are ready for worship.

Anthony, who is unfamiliar with this church's particular protocol, courageously marches up front for the children's sermon with his cousins following him. The pastor takes on the daunting job of explaining Pentecost to preschool and kindergarten minds, puzzling Pentecost with its tongues of fire and the Holy Spirit coming into lives partly because Jesus left earth and partly because we need him so much. The man connects. He focuses on beginnings and birth, saying that Pentecost is the Holy Spirit's birthday in much the same way as Christmas is Jesus' birthday. As his show-and-tell clincher, he lights a birthday candle in honor of the Holy Spirit, then dismisses the children.

But Anthony stays up front. He engages the pastor in a one-on-one conversation that everyone watches but no one hears. I wonder what kind of theological comment or question our grandson has on his mind and whether it's worthy of holding up the entire service. The dialogue lasts for a couple of interchanges and then ends with the pastor giving Anthony the little candle. Anthony turns around, comes up the church aisle, stops at our row, leans across two people, and hands me the candle without a word. Then he continues out of the sanctuary, scurrying to catch up with the other children on their way to children's church.

After the service, the pastor quotes Anthony's side of the conversation to us: "Do you think you could give me that candle? It's my grandma's birthday today too."

I look down at the wax cylinder with its protruding wick—still in my hand. It once burned with a little tongue of fire in a holy place. I shall keep it forever.

Holy Spirit, we admit to wondering who you are and where you are and how you work. Thank you for the metaphors of fire and wind that help us feel you burn and blow through our lives. Thank you for being our candle in the dark. Amen.

PART THREE

CHILD-EYED CREATION

"God who made you has something to say to you . . .
For I will pour water on the thirsty ground
and send streams coursing through the parched earth.
I will pour my Spirit into your descendants
and my blessing on your children."

Isaiah 44:2-3

15

CREATION: DAY SIX

*So God formed from the dirt of the ground all the animals of the field and all
the birds of the air. He brought them to the Man to see what he would name
them. Whatever the Man called each living creature, that was its name.*

Genesis 2:19-20

Two-year-old Josiah sits in our kitchen booth. Alongside him on the
bench is a miniature Red Flyer wagon full of play animals. They are
a hodgepodge of leftovers from our own children's childhoods, good
deals from garage sales, hand-me-downs from cousins, and occasional
new purchases by a grandparent tempted to add to the overflow.

Some of the animals are rubbery and soft; others are hard plastic
replicas, skinny and skeletal. Animals and birds from both the farm
and the jungle hunker down together. Even the lion and the lamb
rub noses in the crowded wagon.

Josiah picks up each animal, studies it briefly, and improvises. He
takes the horse on a roller-coaster ride through the air as he invents
the sound that a toddler thinks a flying horse makes. Then he plops
it into place along the table's edge. When he marches the elephant
across the table terrain, I imagine thunderous footsteps coming down
on Africa's dry plains. He gives the monkeys exuberant arm motions
as he chatters for them; he hoots mournfully for the fat, motionless
owl. After each one's onstage debut, Josiah carefully positions it in
the lengthening parade of animals.

As he sets each creature down, he names it: Horse, Doggie, Jaff,
Zebra, Potamus, Kitty-Cat, Yi-Yon. He is unfamiliar with the llama.
He calls it Sheep-Camel and then smiles. Then he methodically
knocks each one of them over, shouting, "Kaboom!" after each hit,
followed by a singsong "Na-night" as he sees them prone. There they

lie, all of creation resting on the seventh day.

Then Josiah shifts his strategy. This time during the forty-animal lineup, he calls each of them Bunny. "That's not a bunny; that's a giraffe," I say. But he persists. Pick up a creature; call it Bunny (forty times); chuck it into the wagon. My questions surface: *Is he simply being a stubborn two-year-old? Or is he just tuckered out, his memory for names drained for the day?* I want to correct, coddle, or comfort him; I want to change the way this scene is ending.

I wonder how God could simply sit by and watch when he brought his newly created animals to Adam. Did he question whether Adam would name them correctly? Did he require Adam to observe their sounds and actions so that their names would fit them? Was he concerned Adam would get bored? Repeat himself? Quit? Did God have some kind of veto for a name like Platypus?

Actually, I think he just watched the parade and smiled.

Creator God, thank you for all of your amazing birds and beasts, for the farmyard noises and jungle sounds, and for the child play that they inspire. Thank you for your trust in us to care for your creation, for your delight in the way we enjoy the whole parade, and for your flexibility and forgiveness when we don't always get it right. Amen.

16

Noticing

Job, are you listening? Have you noticed all this? . . .
Do you have any idea how God does it all . . .
How he piles up the cumulus clouds —
all these miracle-wonders of a perfect Mind?
He orders the snow, "Blanket the earth!"
and the rain, "Soak the whole countryside!"
No one can escape the weather — it's there.
And no one can escape from God.

Job 37:14-16,6-7

Jack notices. From five years of earth experience, he knows enough about clouds and water and temperature to report his findings often. He believes that the older generation can benefit from his scientific discoveries. As a child, I would lie on a grassy patch of ground and label cloud shapes. These days, Jack invites me to join him on the trampoline for an elevated look at the cloud-studded skies. I climb aboard. Between jumps and gasps on this breezy day, he points upward and says, "There's a rusty old car. And here come some more wheels. Another rusty one. There must be a junkyard up there." During a break, we lie down on the trampoline and look skyward again. Jack notices that God has changed the patterns and informs me of these new identities. "There's a green, wrinkly, gi-mongous monster. And I see an elephant. There's an island. And there's a tornado. Look, Grandma, a very fat alligator eating a big egg off of a planet!"

Noticing what Jack notices takes patience — interminable waits of doing nothing while he, who has all the time in the world, imagines and shouts out the video titles of his slow-motion sky movie.

Jack also believes that the water from clouds was designed

especially for boys bent on doing lab experiments. When I ask him why there is a wad of gum left in a cup of water on my workbench, he explains, "'Cause I want to chew it again, and if you put it in water, it doesn't stick to anything and you can just pop it into your mouth. Sam and I figured this out by 'espearmunt.' We hid our gum behind the Tupperware. It got really stuck. When we put it in the bathtub and blew water at it through a shot-thingy, green bubbles stuck to the gum, but the gum didn't stick to anything!"

Later, over lunch, we discuss the weather. Jack decides this is a teaching moment; Grandma has much to learn about analyzing day-to-day forecasts. Jumbles of ideas tumble and stutter from his mouth. He talks slowly, repeats his sentences, starts several times but often loses the tail end, as if his ideas were pollywogs hoping to be frogs someday. I want to finish his sentences for him. Instead, I move into a long-listening mode and take notes. Later, when I sort out his data, I notice he has invented a new meteorology continuum.

"Okay, Grandma. It's this way." He stretches out his arms and labels his left hand "very hot" and his right hand "very cold." He nods at his left hand and says, "That's a minus two, like how your bare piggies feel on a very hot deck. Minus one is when you are wearing shorts and your legs touch metal. Zero is when you're in a nice warm house or a nice warm car." He moves his left hand closer toward his right.

I respond with the attentiveness of a good student: "What's a number one, Jack?"

"That's when your hands get like the inside of a refrigerator. And number two is when you feel like you're holding two giant icicles in each hand."

"And number three?"

"You're freezing—like being inside of an ice pack! And four is you're in the Arctic in a really cold ice cave with no clothes on."

Jack needs a control-study volunteer. Just then, Great-Grandma walks into the house from her afternoon walk. "Great-Grandma," Jack asks, "how cold is it outside?"

"My hands are cold, Jack, like they've been in a refrigerator!"

There you have it: scientific proof that five-year-olds have the inside track into God's creation intricacies . . . because they notice.

God of this earth, thank you for nature's artistry and complexity. Thank you that your creation engages children with wonder and teaches us to look again at clouds and water and weather in ways we have not seen them before. Amen.

17

BEAUTY AND THE BUTTERFLY

I'm asking GOD for one thing, only one thing:
To live with him in his house my whole life long.
I'll contemplate his beauty; I'll study at his feet. . . .
I'm sure now I'll see God's goodness in the exuberant earth.

Psalm 27:4,13

July. Family vacation. We watch from our lounging places under shade trees as our children revisit their childhoods. They wade in the creek, build a tree fort, swing in the hammock, canoe, play ball, and fling fish lines. They invite their spouses, their offspring, their siblings, my husband and me, and other assorted kin to play along with them. "Let's build a dam in the creek so the water gurgles louder." "How do we put a second story on the tree house?" "Who wants to go fishing with me?" "We need someone to referee this game."

At one point our youngest son shouts, "Here. Take care of my baby!" Our youngest grandson lands in my lap as his father grabs a net and, with legs leaping and arms flailing, chases a yellow swallowtail butterfly through the yard, over the creek bridge, and into the meadow. Another son, inspired by his brother, calls on his high school track experience as a sprinter to join the chase, runs nearly a quarter of a mile on his midlife legs, then correctly times, between tired puffs, a wild, far-reaching swoop of his net and catches beauty midair. I am caught in flashbacks and time warp. These grown men were little once, like our grandchildren who now catch the contagion and chase butterflies with their dads. How good of God to stamp "Repeat" on generational moments—to let us relive what we could not retain.

I watch the return-to-childhood saga continue as our oldest son once again fills the position of preplanner. He stands ready with form-aldehyde, garnered through research and hospital privileges, to put the butterflies to sleep. He has read books on making insect displays and is ready with the supplies: frames, cotton backing, pins, and labels. He teaches as he creates: "This is how the anesthetic works. This is how to carefully spread their wings. Catch two of the same kind so you can study the color design on front and back. See how that one has a furry antenna, different from all the others?"

Our daughter weaves through all the activity, just as she did when she was a little girl outnumbered by noisy brothers. She observes keenly, arranges children so they can better see the display, gathers nets for further distribution, inserts encouraging comments when enthusiasm ebbs, and brings out the snacks.

I, as always, ponder the questions: *What motivates us to chase after things? Why can't we be childlike more often? Why does time slip by so mercilessly? What emptiness in us longs to capture beauty? Why do our children have to grow up?*

The gorgeous butterfly display now sits on the mantel. This is obviously God's handiwork. We look at each wing and color and antenna again. I turn to look at the lookers—these grandchildren and adult children gathered round—and view hair and limbs, expressions and personality. Shimmering awe puddles at the base of my heart, where I see God's reflection.

God of generations, thank you for babies and butterflies, proof that you delight in beauty and endless individuality, that you want this world to go on for our benefit and for your praise. Help us catch our mortal breaths more often and exhale our hallelujahs heavenward. Amen.

18

DANDELIONS

God himself is right alongside to keep you steady and on track until things
are all wrapped up by Jesus. God, who got you started in this spiritual
adventure . . . will never give up on you.
Never forget that.

1 Corinthians 1:8-9

Daffodils and dandelions rise from beds and lawns this April shouting, "Good morning!" to spring, sending bugle calls to the rest of creation. I rejoice that the daffodil bulbs Orv, my husband, planted have grown; I wonder how the dandelions he sprayed have managed to persevere. I begin to suspect that yellow in any form has a message.

Today I see my champagne-colored van as pale yellow. I drive with two of my grandsons in the backseat and listen to their comments on the passing landscape as they megaphone information to me on our ride home. "Look at that traffic light, Grandma. It's swinging in the wind. It's yellow, Grandma, slow down." They point out clumps of daffodils at intersections and dandelions in several lawns: "Look at all those yellow flowers! I'll bet there's a billion of 'em." Obviously, the broad-leaf weed killer was ineffective in other spots, too.

After rounding another corner, one small tour guide announces, "That house needs some paint, that's for sure."

"What color would you paint it, Caleb, if you could choose?"

"Yellow," he says without hesitation. I am not surprised. Yellow has been Caleb's favorite color since he turned three and learned his colors. He has not wavered in the four years since, committing more than half his lifetime to loving yellow.

Our interchange reminds me of a book his mother (my daughter) gave me for my sixtieth birthday called *The Persistence of Yellow*, by Monique Duval:[11]

> You ask me how things work. I think of endless cycles, the hum and spin of everything. So I tell you this: hold the pale green stalk up high. And then run hard so the wind will catch the wings of the dandelion seeds. Let them fall like sparks, like stars, back to the earth. . . . That's all there is to it: The persistence of yellow.

Yellow is that way—it has staying power. Kind of like God, I think: enduring, beautiful, and bright with hope. Perhaps next time we go riding, my grandsons and I will each collect a fistful of dandelions that have gone to seed, then hold them outside the champagne-yellow van's windows and watch them detach like wisps of angels into the air, eventually landing alongside our quarter-mile driveway. After all, we want to do our part to celebrate and perpetuate yellow.

But should we tell their grandpa?

Our faithful God, yellow colors the sun that comes up every morning, paints the dandelions and daffodils every spring, and opens the eyes of our children and grandchildren. We thank you for your persistent reminders that you will never give up on us. Amen.

19

GREEN

Good people will prosper like palm trees,
Grow tall like Lebanon cedars; transplanted to GOD's courtyard,
They'll grow tall in the presence of God, lithe and green,
virile still in old age.

Psalm 92:13-14

Jack prepares for preschool on Tuesday and Thursday mornings.

"Jack, do you have your shirt on yet?" His mother's question aims its way down the hallway toward the bedroom, only to find a little boy trying to tunnel a matchbox-sized race car through an inside-out sleeve.

"Jack, where did you put your shoes last night?" She finds them buried in the box of Legos, between alien spaceships and pirate schooners.

The winter months of predawn awakening are past; the sluggish dressing-in-the-dark with a mother's promptings are over. Spring moves Jack from lollygagging and the lethargy of staying undressed to a new phase of self-help determination. He wants to dress himself. Khaki trousers go on, but backward. It becomes possible to put a shirt on sideways. His parents are grateful for Velcro on shoes that replaces the shoestrings of their youth.

At a quarter to nine, mother and son are out the door, entering the Jeep, fastening seat belts on the car seat, and rejoicing that they are on their way. This particular morning, the foliage is doing resurrection acts in its outdoor theatre. Jack becomes an audience of one. Staring out the jeep window, he shares his heartfelt thoughts with his mother: "I just love green. It's my favorite color." On this moving stage, he sees dark-shadowed evergreens, bushes frothing with the chartreuse of new buds, spiky grasses pushing kelly green up through the earth. Green drapes itself over brown everywhere he looks.

"Green makes me smile," he says reverently.

Surely the Creator is pleased that a small boy has heard his voice and been touched by spring's drama. God shows Jack an encore: the bright green veins in newborn leaves, meadow green in vacant lots, lime shafts holding up crocuses and daffodils, ground covers of mint and sage.

Jack stops talking for several minutes. Miles pass.

"I just don't think I can keep smiling," he says apologetically. "My face is tired."

But the show goes on. The green keeps coming, keeps going by the backseat window. Jack wishes his smiling muscles would not give out.

I remember asking an artist friend once what she was painting that day. She replied with an ecstasy that I didn't quite understand at the time: "I didn't paint a picture today, but, oh did I ever learn a lot about the color green!"

Jack helps me get it. So does the apostle Paul through his benediction to young and old Romans:

May the God of green hope fill you up with joy, fill you up with peace, so that your believing lives, filled with the life-giving energy of the Holy Spirit, will brim over with hope! (15:13)

Creator God, thank you that little children and old people are forever green in your eyes, trees with leaves that never wither. Your resurrection presence makes us prosper and grow at age four or a hundred and four. Thank you. Amen.

20
THE FALL

And now to him who can keep you on your feet, standing tall in his bright presence, fresh and celebrating—to our one God, our only Savior, through Jesus Christ, our Master, be glory, majesty, strength, and rule before all time, and now, and to the end of all time. Yes.

Jude 24-25

Josiah rocks his torso back and forth in the stiff and stable Adirondack chair, trying to turn the chair into something it is not: a rocking chair. Its sturdy wood and flat feet do not cooperate. He jumps from the chair and says, "Grandma, pull the chair out." Instinctively he knows that rocking chairs do not do well up against a wall. I apologize for the Adirondack. "It doesn't rock, Josiah. Sorry."

That afternoon I rock Josiah's baby brother, Malakai, to sleep. I repeat the motions and cradling and awe of rocking parents and grandparents through the ages. I rearrange his blanket to make him feel more secure, putting the satin edging that he often fingers for comfort into his little hand, the same edging that his other grandmother lovingly hand-stitched to the flannel just before she died. I look down at him sleeping, at his profile of little nose and soft cheeks and eyelashes, and wonder, *Is there anything more beautiful on the face of this old earth than a baby's face?* In this moment, I couldn't agree more with God's choice to overcome an ugly world through the birth of a Baby.

I sing "Rock-a-Bye, Baby" to my grandchild, this tiny type of Christ, the lilting melody sounding tender as a lullaby should. After the third repetition, though, I hear a roughness in the lyrics that I had not paid attention to before:[12]

Rock-a-bye baby on the treetop
When the wind blows the cradle will rock.
When the bough breaks the cradle will fall,
And down will come baby, cradle and all.

Why have we sung these traumatic lyrics to our children for generations? Has the familiar tune played cover-up for the damage and
destruction in the lullaby's lines? I go to the Internet and discover
that the words were written by a pilgrim in 1872: Effie Crockett
(related to Davy). Perhaps she had noticed how Indian women hung
their babies from a tree to rock in the wind and wanted to pen a
warning about choosing a good strong bough.

On the other hand, perhaps unknowingly, or maybe deliberately,
Effie Crockett included some theological truth in her lyrics: When
the winds of the Spirit blow and a person is right with God, all is well
with the world and the treetops. However, when Eve ate that piece
of fruit, the bough did break, and down fell humanity, immortality
and all. Adam and Eve fell that Genesis day, and ever since, so does
every baby.

When eleven-month-old Malakai wakes up from his nap, he continues his course in Footwork 101, believing in the idea of walking,
though he seems too shaky to do so. After a few successful baby steps,
he stumbles over his own three-and-a-half-inch foot and slams face-
first into the Adirondack's hardwood bench, smashing his cheekbone
before thudding to the floor. I cannot catch this falling baby in time.
His cries serrate my heart as my head spins with possibilities: stitches,
a black eye, scarring, concussion, blindness. *Why wasn't I able to catch
him, to keep him from falling, to save him from hurt?* I hold this bleed-
ing baby, both of us longing for comfort.

Malakai's beautiful baby cheek scabs over the next day. He is
marred from the fall. We all are. I rock him to sleep again with a
more promising lullaby:[13]

Jesus loves me! He who died
Heaven's gate to open wide;

He will wash away my sin,
Let His little child come in.

Thank you, Jesus, for your painful descent to rescue each of us from fall-
ing. A baby who becomes our Savior! We will never understand the
miracle, we will never exhaust the mystery, until you rock us to sleep in
your everlasting arms and wake us to walk steadily across the floors of
mansions you have prepared for us. Amen.

21

Joy

I've found the recipe for being happy whether full or hungry, hands full or hands empty. Whatever I have, wherever I am, I can make it through anything in the One who makes me who I am.

Philippians 4:12-13

Joy is my middle name—literally and, for the most part, truly. When our four children were little and exhausting, I remember describing to a friend that I felt a deep, underlying joy, but that it was a tired joy, as physical demands and spiritual promises jostled within me during those active parenting days.

Our children and grandchildren gallivant together the first week of July in a cabin compound deep in Montana's wilderness, too many miles from any grocery store to "just pick up some mayonnaise." Tiredness and joy coexist again as four generations work and play to reach their vacation goals: no one starves, no one gets injured beyond a one-Band-Aid solution, and no one says, "I'm bored."

Nine children, eight and under, frolic through the week. They stumble onto gifts: A two-year-old pulls wild daisies out by the roots and gives them as a love offering to a great-grandmother (my mother) resting on the porch; upon catching a wiggling trout, two seven-year-olds break into "God Bless America" from their paddleboat on the lake; a five-year-old lies on the dock and watches fingerlings form schools in the clear water.

"Know why fish swim in schools, Grandma?" Jack asks.

"I've wondered about that, Jack. Do you know?" I ask him.

"Because they're all together in a clump and they stay that way and no one leaves the group," he explains, plumbing his preschool experience. The next day he looks again for the underwater class-rooms. "There's no schools today, Grandma," he says sadly. "I think we must have caught the teacher and the substitute yesterday."

Mid-afternoon on the Fourth of July, grandson Emmett's mom gathers the children for a scavenger hunt. She divides the cousins into two teams, assigns leaders, and gives each group a list:

> 3 round rocks
> 1 pinecone
> 4 blades of grass
> 1 daisy
> Grandma's middle name
> 1 little wooden boat
> 1 purple flower
> 1 life jacket
> a stick as long as this _____

To leader Sam she hands a plastic tackle box to hold the treasures; to leader Anthony she gives a small wooden box with a dowel handle. She surveys the setup, feels their eagerness, and then remembers that the last entry on the list, a life jacket, won't fit inside a box.

"If something doesn't fit into your container, just carry it with you," their aunt instructs. "When you're all finished finding every-thing on your list, meet me at the front porch."

The leadership styles differ. Sam has a come-along approach and invites his young cousins to hang together like a pack of wolves as they search for one treasure at a time. Anthony, on the other hand, assigns rocks to one, blades of grass to another, and encourages his teammates to go their separate ways. Periodically, both teams check their scavenger hunt list again. Several times a grandchild breaks away, comes to me, and asks, "What's your middle name, Grandma?" I whisper, "Joy," into each little listening ear.

I watch as one group gathers under a pine tree to account for all their treasures before running to the porch finish line. "Here's the purple flower," one announces. "Is this rock round enough?" another asks as he plunks it into the box. "I found the pinecone," brags another. And then I overhear their young leader ask, "How are we going to get Joy into this box?"

Carry it with you, my grandchildren. Carry it with you.

Dear God of joy, thank you that the prize our daughter-in-law chose for our scavenger hunters was to light their Fourth of July sparklers early, before nightfall. Thank you for running, gleeful children holding fireworks above their heads, threading through each other in spontaneous choreography, dancing for joy in the tradition of your psalmist. Amen.

PART FOUR

GOD'S LOVE

So I never lose sight of your love,
But keep in step with you, never missing a beat. . . .
then join hands with the others in the great circle,
dancing around your altar, GOD,
Singing God-songs at the top of my lungs,
telling God-stories.

Psalm 26:3,6-7

22

BELOVED

Long before [God] laid down earth's foundations, he had us in mind, had settled on us as the focus of his love, to be made whole and holy by his love. Long, long ago he decided to adopt us into his family through Jesus Christ.

Ephesians 1:4-5

Our Janelle has had a baby boy. She and her husband live in the Washington, DC, area; we are in Washington State. She phones us just before midnight Thursday, western time, and tells us he arrived in the early morning hours of what is already Friday, east coast time. We experience grandparental whiplash trying to wrap our minds around a back-to-the-future time warp and the shock of a first grandchild. Very soon we make a cross-country journey to hold him — to make sure he is real and in real time.

At the airport, our daughter places her blanket bundle into my receiving arms, all five pounds, three ounces of him. I am feeling oh so maternal again, my muscles and skin and heart recalling tucked-away memories of cradling. From a deep soul place, something wells up within me, filling my lungs with a liquid love. I cannot breathe. He is stunning. Intense dark eyes, a chin dimple, shocks of black hair that account for at least one of his ounces.

We take him home to the apartment. The obvious is obvious once again: A newborn takes up your whole life. Janelle and I get nothing done for days except keeping the little guy alive through feedings and burpings and diaper changings and comfortings so he won't cry his lungs out. I watch the new parents drape themselves with a cloak of care that nearly smothers them. Miraculously, they keep on breathing.

Apart from showing up, baby Anthony has done nothing to

deserve love. We don't even know him well enough to know what or whom we love. When he wets and dirties and interrupts the night, when he demands time and attention and suckling without any consideration for the adult agendas, he gets loved anyway. We put our lives on hold to hold him.

My shoulders ache while holding him, not from the five pounds plus of weight bearing but from practicing the discipline of gentleness: giving hugs that will not crush him and kisses that will not leave permanent imprints on his delicate cheeks. I forget to put my emotions in check, however. My brain stem tells my tear ducts to cry because of the thoughts I have about God's love for one tiny baby and his grandmother. I soak in the adverbs that describe how God loves: unconditionally, sacrificially, spontaneously, and much. Yes, Anthony, I love you in all those ways too.

At 2 a.m., while rocking him to sleep in one arm, my other hand is free to take a book from the shelf. I open it randomly. Henri Nouwen speaks to me from *Life of the Beloved*:

Long before any human being saw us, we are seen by God's loving eyes. Long before anyone heard us cry or laugh, we are heard by our God who is all ears for us. Long before any person spoke to us in this world, we are spoken to by the voice of eternal love. Our preciousness, uniqueness and individuality are not given us by [parents and grandparents] who meet us in clock-time—our brief chronological existence—but by the One who has chosen us with an ever-lasting love, a love that existed from all eternity and will last through all eternity.[14]

Our loving God, thank you for this first grandchild. When Anthony learns to call us Grandpa and Grandma, we will have waited more than fifty years for those names to be ours. Thank you that the very moment Anthony was conceived, with no waiting at all you called him beloved. Hallelujah! Amen.

23

COLORED COPY

You're here to be light, bringing out the God-colors in the world. God is not a secret to be kept.

Matthew 5:14

Sam shows up on our doorstep with a grin that resembles a surprised alligator. He is free from first grade for the day (something about St. Patrick's Day and teachers' work day all rolled into one, his mother explains). His two feet jump over the threshold, kick off shoes, and make a left turn into the kitchen.

After the usual kitchen-table artwork session, Sam vanishes. I find him in the loft, wedged between my desk and the copy machine. He wants to color-copy his drawing of elves collecting silver bricks in a Conestoga wagon by the light of a lavender moon. I explain that our ancient Canon copier makes only black-and-white copies, no color. "But a night scene may just come out all right anyway," I say when I read his disappointment. We experiment. We look for tinges of color. There are none.

I encourage him to add colors to the black-and-white copy with his felt pens. He does so, trying to turn the gray of the moon back to lavender and the black of the elves' clothing into its former red. His work reminds me of the tinting procedure that a technician did to my high school graduation picture, a cotton-swab-and-dye procedure designed to make the sepia photo more lifelike by coloring my eyes and sweater a matching shade of blue. Sam is disappointed in his attempts to resurrect his black-and-white drawing. It still looks lifeless. He requests that I go to Kinko's and pay for a colored copy. I promise him that I will on Friday.

I ask Sam if he has ever seen black-and-white television. He hasn't. Years ago, after I told a friend about God's love, she began to see "God colors" in a world that for her had been dully tinted. She said the change was like switching from an old twelve-inch black-and-white TV to a big-screen colored one.

Sam wants color. He's on to something.

Dear Jesus, light up our lives so that we can be the crayons that scribble your secrets everywhere. Amen.

24

STORYBOOKS

Keep your eyes on Jesus. . . . *When you find yourselves flagging in your faith,
go over that story again, item by item, that long litany of hostility he plowed
through. That* will *shoot adrenaline into your souls!*

Hebrews 12:2-3

Our eldest son, Keith, and his wife, Cindy, collected children's books
during the nine years before their first baby was born. Their hobby
played well with their poverty. For low-cost entertainment, they rum-
maged through love-worn books on Saturday afternoon forays into
garage and library sales, Goodwill and Salvation Army stores. For a few
hours, they would retreat from the higher learning of heavy graduate
texts and find rest in elementary language and whimsical illustrations.
They rejoiced every time they found an out-of-print book that was a
favorite from their own childhoods. Familiar characters engaged them
after years of being shelved: Little Miss Suzy, Scuttle, Zachary Zween,
Alexander. Each used storybook came with the vision of opening the
cover in front of their own listening child at bedtime someday.

By the time sons Sam and Jack came into their lives, Keith and
Cindy had a priceless collection of a thousand well-chosen volumes.
Three books a day for a year. A thousand stories expressively presented
and eagerly digested. Word meals served on paper book "plates;" toddler vocabulary snacks and preschool plot picnics taken in with every
slow turning of a page.

"Read me a story, Mommy." "Story time, Daddy!" The pictures
stay still in front of them — long enough for little eyes to eat and swal-
low, for minds to chew, for memories to bite. Intermittently, for a
change in the menu, the family goes to the library for more take-home
food. The book banquet continues.

Sometimes Orv and I take our turn at reading these stories to our grandchildren. We muse about how we have been fed by the Bible over the years and how those same plot tensions keep appearing in nearly every storybook: good versus bad, distress before rescue, the ups and downs and reversals of moving toward the happy ending. We admit the need to revisit and taste that Word daily for reminders about what God is up to.

Preschooler Jack revisits a story one day. When he can't keep up with older brother Sam and his friends, he whines that they run faster, swim faster, even eat faster. His dad, remembering a childhood favorite, reads him the saga of Zachary Zween, an upbeat reversal lesson about the last becoming first and, by the end of the story, the most blessed:

> Albert Ames went first each day,
> Because his name began with A.
> For A to Z, that was the rule
> Of this particular London school.
> And who came last?
> Poor Zachary Zween —
> So envious that his face turned green![15]

Zachary hates the alphabet, the rhyme goes on to say, until he figures out that being last in line floats him into unexpected adventures: helping a cat, picking a buttercup, and being the enviable chosen one to ride in a caboose.

Jack quietly takes it all in. His dad asks if he understands how being last could be better than always being first.

"Sometimes it doesn't feel like it," he admits. "I have to wait."

Inwardly, I agree. Sometimes stories take a while to digest.

Dear God, you have authored thousands and thousands of life stories, each one unique. You have deemed your collection worth saving, pouring out your love for us in your larger-than-life salvation story. Thank you for the nourishment we receive from the old, old stories of the past and the new ones of today. Tell us another one, Father. Your children are listening. Amen.

25
FRIENDS

"This is my command: Love one another the way I loved you. This is the very best way to love. Put your life on the line for your friends. You are my friends when you do the things I command you. . . . You didn't choose me, remember; I chose you."

John 15:12-13,16

Two-year-old Josiah has great friend-choosing capacities. When he arrives at our house, the first thing on his agenda is to go to The Toy Room and choose one or two companions for the day. Plastic figurine Jessie, girl cowboy of *Toy Story* fame, won at least a month of loyal visits. Pooh Bear and Piglet often keep him company as he navigates the pretend hundred-acre wood inside our home. Lately he has been spending time with Ernie, the thatch-haired puppet from *Sesame Street* who wears a blue and orange striped shirt, and Camel, a promotional toy from the movie *The Prince of Egypt*.

For weeks now, every visit comes with two initial questions: "Where's Ernie? Where's Camel?" They get tucked in alongside him under his blanket at naptime. They bounce on the trampoline with him while he giggles at their antics. They ride in the pockets of his bib overall. They sit on his high chair tray during snack time and compete with him for raisins and Cheerios. They watch videos with him. They are never out of his hands or sight.

I do not understand his choice of friends. Jessie's paint has worn off her hard plastic shell, and she offers no softness for cuddling. I find Pooh Bear and Piglet pretty bland, actually — a faded pair of over-advertised storybook characters. The Ernie-and-Camel combination leaves me stymied. What an odd couple! An intelligence-challenged puppet and a royalty-bearing beast. How did Josiah decide they belong together?

But then, why does Jesus choose any of us?

Take me, for instance: logic-challenged, touchy-feely, bones creaking and muscles aching, eyesight failing, tension knots in my neck, and an inability to complete every day's to-do list. Pair me with my husband, a man who starts more projects than he can ever finish, has backaches and a knee out of joint, ignores the world around him while watching a baseball game, and is sometimes impatient.

And then there's Josiah: incontinent, messy when eating, whiny when tired, illiterate, demanding, and unemployable.

Jesus loves us, although it doesn't make any sense.

We are never out of his hands or out of his sight.

Dear Jesus, thank you for choosing us as friends even though we differ so much from you, lack admirable qualities, and give you little in return. Thank you that you are with us always, loyal forever. Amen.

26
SEPARATION ANXIETY

"I am the Vine, you are the branches. When you're joined with me and I with you, the relation intimate and organic, the harvest is sure to be abundant. Separated, you can't produce a thing."

John 15:5-6

Some of our grandchildren are going through a "clinging vine" phase. One little grandson cannot bear to have his Bob the Builder video separated from his clutches to go into a DVD player, where it disappears from his sight. He doesn't watch his videos; he simply holds them close.

Yesterday I took three-year-old Josiah to his second swimming lesson at the aquatic center. After changing him into his red-orange swimsuit, we began moving out of the dressing room. He wailed when he saw the pool; he wailed again when he saw Teacher Mary. "I want to go bye-bye," he announced and then panic-crawled up into my arms. I held him in a tight embrace, trying to save him from fear and separation. "Grandma will hold you, Josiah. Don't cry."

Last week's separation anxiety occurred when Josiah's bedtime-cuddler Ezra (the softest toy dog in four counties) was left in our Suburban. Josiah had lived through one night without his companion, surviving on his parents' promises that they'd retrieve Ezra the next day. But his parents forgot. At 4:30 a.m. we got the "I feel like such a bad parent" distress call: "Dad, Josiah's been crying for Ezra for an hour. It's not a disobedience cry; it's an 'I really miss him' cry. I think he'll stop sobbing if I put him in his car seat and tell him we are going to get Ezra from Grandpa and Grandma's house. Could you put Ezra on the front porch so we don't wake you up again?"

The next day we received an e-mail from our daughter-in-law

Donna-Lea reporting that the third-floor neighbors in their apartment building moved back to Germany. Four-year-old Emmett had said an uncomfortable good-bye to his friend Niklas as he watched his mother cry over her pending separation from Niklas's mother, Angelika. Farewell frustrations oozed between the lines of Emmett's conversation hours later: "Do you know what comes from God's mouth? People do. Kids and grown-ups," he blurted. "He has a wide mouth. He has the widest mouth in the world. It's H-U-G-E!"

Emmett continued his comfort treatise on separation anxiety: "And the workers build new houses. That's what God wants, so his people have places to live."

"Where does God live, Emmett?" his mother asked.

"He lives far away. He doesn't live in our world." And then, after a long pause, "He lives in Germany. Don't tell anyone."

Later he hid himself and his grief in the laundry hamper. His mother heard him hollering through the lid at high decibels, "Do you miss your friend Angelika, Mama?" And then, even louder, "I am your friend now." Not a bad offer from a small son's heart.

Our Anthony enters a school new to him at the beginning of third grade. He looks for a soul mate to shorten the time of loneliness between the leaving and the starting over. His parents arrange an early September overnight birthday party and invite five of his new classmates. Between wild excitement and boyish chaos, their interaction looks like a fast-forward version of catch and release. Even when each boy lies down on the mats arranged like the spokes of a wheel on the family room floor, their heads hubbed together, they have little capacity for quietly connecting before they fall asleep. Anthony learns that getting to know someone and being known by another takes a long time. After the party is over, with a patient yearning he tells his mother, "Mom, I just want a friend to always be by my side."

Without knowing it, Anthony has echoed a down-through-the-ages description of Jesus—the friend who will always be by his side, who will never leave or forsake him.

'Tis a good thing to cling to the Vine.

Vine-dressing God, as you graft us into yourself and heal the separations that break our human hearts, keep inviting us to cling to you and feel the tendrils of your Vine-love binding us close. Dependent branches that we are, we thank you for the promise that we can never be separated from your love. Amen.

27

REQUESTS

"Don't bargain with God. Be direct. Ask for what you need. This is not a cat-and-mouse, hide-and-seek game we're in. If your little boy asks for a serving of fish, do you scare him with a live snake on his plate? If your little girl asks for an egg, do you trick her with a spider? As bad as you are, you wouldn't think of such a thing—you're at least decent to your own children. And don't you think the Father who conceived you in love will give the Holy Spirit when you ask him?"

Luke 11:10-13

Many of the people I went to grade school with more than fifty years ago are grandparents now. I run into an old classmate at a wedding reception and begin talking about this mutual playground of grandparenting we find ourselves cavorting in. He and his wife live on a fertile acreage near the rural town where we all grew up, and they have begun raising sheep for their city-bound grandchildren as a way of show-and-telling them about farming and animal husbandry and God's good creatures.

"My grandson calls me Bop," he announces between bites of wedding cake. "Short for Boppa, I guess. He's in pre-K. Can you believe these kids nowadays have two years of preschool and then kindergarten? When I started first grade, I couldn't even write my own name. The other day Jackson phones me and says, "Bop, I need Rambo. We're on the letter R next week. Can you bring him down for show-and-tell on Thursday?"

"What's a grandfather to say when his grandson makes such a request?" asks Bop.

Our table of aging listeners choruses in unison, "You say yes, of course."

Jackson's preschool alphabet book featured a ram for R week. His five-year-old mind immediately thought of Rambo in his grandfather's sheep pen. Rambo, whose ingrown horn was lovingly cut by deft, experienced hands so that it is curling well now. Rambo, whose offspring are called Jacob-sheep because they are mottled and spotted like the sheep Jacob inherited from his father-in-law, Laban, in the Genesis story. Rambo, who has never been on a two-hour ride into the city.

But when Bop learns that a dear friend's funeral is scheduled for that same Thursday, he regretfully phones his daughter. He gives her the sad news that Rambo cannot come to preschool after all and asks her to break the news as gently as possible to Jackson.

Hours later, in an effort to comfort her father and appease her son, she phones. "Dad," she says, "all is not lost! Next week is the letter S, which stands for sheep."

What's a father to do? A grandson's three-word request, "I need Rambo," initiates a mountain of preparation. During the next week, love motivates Bop as he puts fresh straw bedding in his covered trailer, creatively cordons off pens for safety in travel and showmanship upon arrival, figures out food-and-water strategies, scoops, and cleans. On the following Thursday he entices Rambo, a ewe, and three sheep into the trailer and heads for the city. The mobile sheep home has a front side door and a large back opening. The preschool children file through in less than fifteen minutes. They are enthralled. Jackson is proud. His mother is grateful.

As Bop ends his story, we finish our last bites of wedding cake. Our attention shifts to the bride and groom as they walk past our table. But Bop has a postscript: "I'm thinking about getting a pony soon too . . . for my grandkids."

Next year, the grandparent group predicts, Jackson's little brother will be a preschool hero the Thursday his class learns the letter P.

Father, thank you for listening to our prayer requests. "Ask," you keep telling us, "and you shall receive." We can ask the impossible; we cannot overload you. Give us each the faith of a child to trust that you want to move not only sheep but also our mountains because of the love you have for each of us. Amen.

28
THE MESSAGE

A Message. GOD's Word to Israel through Malachi: GOD said,
"I love you."

Malachi 1:1-2

Kurt and Maluhia take turns carrying their infant son into our home for visits. Heavy car carrier and baby land lightly on our foyer floor, nearly weightless, as if angel helpers do the hefting, or our children's gratitude for this child somehow counteracts the laws of gravity. We absorb our youngest grandson's features: the soft roundedness, the lovely contentment, the mystery of genetics.

After several visits I ask Orv, "Have you noticed that every time Malakai comes, whether he's sleeping or wide awake, his arms are raised?" We look for his benediction when he comes through our front door and are not disappointed. His little fists are usually open instead of clenched, his arms lifted up as if to bless us. We imagine him saying, "Peace to you, my grandparents."

In his introduction to the Old Testament book written by the Hebrew prophet Malachi, Eugene Peterson writes, "[Malachi] keeps us on our toes, listening for God, waiting in anticipation for God, ready to respond to God, who is always coming to us."[16] Our Malakai of Hawaiian and Dutch heritage keeps us listening and watching.

As he gets to the crawling stage, Malakai's outstretched arms of blessing also become reaching ones. "Bless and reach," an all-encompassing mission statement for someone so small. What is beyond him propels him. When he moves past our fireplace chimney, his reaching grip finds the highest brick. When he climbs up my temporary storage unit, he stretches for the Post-it note on the top drawer. I rescue my Christmas 2001 label from his grasp before he eats it. Next I find him chewing on the corner of *Theology and Notes*, a magazine he has grabbed from a hard-to-reach shelf.

Crawling at ground level, he is ho-hum content. But when his daddy tosses him into the upper reaches of the living room for a bird's-eye view of the floor he so faithfully traverses, he chortles and gurgles with glee. Someday he will walk, of course. But for now his upper arms wall-climb large boxes and slap their cardboard tops to make drum music. His hands follow an upward dotted line of shiny upholstery tacks until they find the arm of a chair well above eye level. He pulls himself up to a tiptoe stance and strains to see over the edge. He never opens a bottom drawer; instead he pulls on knobs above his head and then tries to reach in for contents that are beyond his grasp.

"Watch this," his mother says as she stands Malakai up against our refrigerator, the door of which holds several homemade magnets glued to shells, polished stones, old Scrabble letters, and wooden word blocks. "He did this at home," she tells us. "We couldn't believe it, so we got out the video camera." Malakai shoves his little tummy against the shiny white door of the appliance, stands on tiptoe, prances to get his bearings, reaches higher than we would have ever predicted, and, with his chubby right hand, pulls a word magnet down to his level.

He plucks the little block from the fridge and victoriously hands it to me. I turn it over to see the word imprinted on his treasure: "Love" is written there.

Little messenger of God, we hear you.

God of all ages, thank you for using the actions and sounds of these, your little ones, to bring us messages from above. They are your mouthpieces even though they know no words; your communicators even though they understand no concepts. Yet they speak and bless and sing of your love. God, be praised! Amen.

PART FIVE

FRESH WONDER

GOD made my life complete
when I placed all the pieces before him. . . .
Now I'm alert to GOD's ways;
I don't take God for granted.
Every day I review the ways he works;
I try not to miss a trick. . . .
GOD rewrote the text of my life
when I opened the book of my heart to his eyes.

Psalm 18:20,22,24

29

TELLING TIME

*My life leaks away, groan by groan; my years fade
out in sighs. . . .
Desperate, I throw myself on you: you are my God!
Hour by hour I place my days in your hand.*

Psalm 31:10,14-15

When I was in grade school, I learned to tell time by figuring out
where the little hand and the big hand were on the clock. I was
taught to report in fractions, approximate at best: "It's half past six"
or "It's quarter to twelve."

In this technological generation, children are far more specific.
My grandchildren look at their giant digital wristwatches and say,
"It's 6:32" or "It's 11:44, Grandma; time to get going."

Watch-wearing Anthony comes to visit sometime in February.
Barely through the front door, with a hug on the run, Anthony
makes his way to the art center of our home: the kitchen table. It is
strewn with paper, scissors, pens, brushes, paints, and the ever-present stickers—all of it holding bright promise for magic or messes.
His hands reach and shuffle eagerly through the piles before he even
sits down.

After this first burst of passion, Anthony settles into a chair
and soon uncovers a sheet of stickers that draws his full attention.
Scriptures written in enticing fonts burst from yellow balloon shapes.
He begins to read—slowly, phonetically—"Sing a new . . . song . . .
to the Lord; he has done won . . . der . . . ful . . . th . . . ings!" (Psalm
98:1, TEV).

I feel my already sagging jaw drop even lower as I hear, for
the first time, Anthony successfully read words from the Bible, a

discovery so delicious I want the drama to continue. I take a closer look at the sticker and see the biblical reference for the verse he has just read: Ps 98:1. Pointing to the abbreviation and numbers, I ask, "What do you think *this* says?"

He stares at it awhile, unable to apply his phonetic attack to this mishmash of symbols. After a very long and thoughtful pause, he answers, "Grandma, I think that's what time it is in heaven right now."

Digital time in a timeless heaven? Now there's a stretch! I think of C. S. Lewis's Narnia, the fantasyland beyond a wardrobe and beyond time in which four children travel. Lewis could write such an adventure because he never lost the capability to transcend time. He once wrote to a child, "You see . . . I don't think age matters so much as people think. Parts of me are still twelve, but I think other parts were already fifty when I was twelve."[17] Anthony and C. S. Lewis remind me that every child has some old wisdom and that every adult can still get lost in wonder.

Our Anthony lives like that—timelessly—while wearing a watch.

Did I ever, in my wildest dreams, think I would be able to tell what time it is in heaven? And now I can. My grandson taught me how.

Infinite God, thank you that, for now, you are the timekeeper of our lives. But when forever comes, you will tell time to disappear. Remind us of that, Father. Comfort us with the certainty that you will gather us into heaven—along with our children and grandchildren—in your good time. Amen.

30
Picnics

We plan the way we want to live,
but only GOD makes us able to live it.

Proverbs 16:9

In times past, a house was prepared for a new paint job this way: The father gathered his tools and his entire family and put them to work scraping. "Use your elbow grease," he would say. Then he would hand out wire brushes, wooden blocks wrapped in sandpaper, and assorted scrapers. If four-year-old Jack had been there, he would have been assigned the lower slat of wooden siding just above the concrete foundation; six-year-old Sam would have gotten the couple of boards above that, all the way around the house. All the siding would be matched to heights and ages. The oldest kids would stand on ladders and scrape upstairs window frames. The mother would bring the sandwiches and lemonade outdoors for a noon picnic on the grass.

Nowadays, the dad rents a power washer and the mom takes her turn at the nozzle. The jets of spray that take the paint off the house could knock a child senseless. So Grandpa and Grandma get grandchildren for the weekend, for safety's sake, while their parents waterblast the family home.

Sam shares the weekend plans that have been going through his head: "Let's take the middle seat out of your van, Grandma, and then go to Boomer's, where the girl comes to your car window." I think of the days when his grandpa and I ordered hot fudge sundaes from a '57 Chevy at Bunk's Drive-In to sweeten up our Friday night dates. "Then when the food comes," Sam continues, "Jack and I and you and Grandpa can all sit on the floor and eat our hamburgers like we're having a picnic."

We agree to feed Sam's imagination and the digestive tracts of two small boys. The middle bench seat comes out of the van, the car seats get anchored to the far backseat, and our grandsons jump in and buckle up. From my passenger seat, I look back across the spacious interior and see two eager faces about to go on their first limo ride to dine out 1950s style.

After a "Who wants what?" interchange with the girl at the drive-in, we all get out of our seats and take our places on the checkered tablecloth I have spread on the van floor. Sitting cross-legged, a four-some can dine well back there, dipping French fries into a communal ketchup pile and letting the hamburger juices drip where they may. The table conversation begins:

"So, Sam, who do you think is getting older faster, you or Grandpa?" I bait.

Sam looks at Grandpa, hesitates, and then says with courage, "Grandpa."

Grandpa does not let the conversation end there. "Sam, think about it a minute. How do you get older?"

Sam does think awhile and then says, "Every time I have a birthday."

"Right," says Grandpa. "And how do I get older?"

"Every time you have a birthday."

"And how often do we have birthdays, Sam?"

"Once a year." Then comes the hundred-watt lightbulb moment: "So we're both getting older at the same time."

"You've got it," says Grandpa, pleased.

With his last bite of hamburger, little brother, Jack, has the final word: "I get older every time I have lunch."

Father of families, the time we have together is short and often sporadic. Help us see and seize opportunities, savor memories, and give you the credit for little drive-in dramas and grandchild/grandparent dynamics. Amen.

31

*"I'm A to Z, the First and the Final, Beginning
and Conclusion."*

Revelation 22:13

We reserve Saturday to help with the renovation of a 1920s fixer-upper. Our daughter and her husband have purchased an old house with redemption in mind. Not wanting to leave us out of the adventure, they have included us in the remodeling job descriptions. Grandpa, dressing the part, looks like Bob the Builder with his plaid shirt and tool belt. I am ready to sacrifice watching Magic School Bus videos with grandchildren in order to wield a paintbrush.

The grandsons opt to help me paint. Anthony uses a tack cloth to wipe off every last speck of dust from an old door balanced on two sawhorses. His moves are deliberate and patient. His younger brother, Caleb, on the other hand, dips his brush into the paint can before the contents are stirred and swoops the heavy drips eagerly toward the waiting door. I try to give "finishing touches" a new meaning before the paint dries into mushy mounds rather than flat surfaces. We talk about our teamwork and how good it will all look when we are done and why Mom wants all the woodwork painted white.

Caleb pouts a little. "I wonder why she didn't choose yellow for any of the rooms."

I cheerfully say, "Just wait until you grow up, Caleb. Then you can buy a house of your own and paint it any color you choose."

"Not if your wife doesn't want it that color," his older brother knowingly chimes in.

"What would you do if your wife wanted blue and you wanted yellow?" I ask.

Anthony answers while Caleb nods in agreement, "I'd argue with her about it until I won, just like I do with Caleb." I grin, silently mulling over the fact that even though brother-to-brother negotiating is good practice, these little boys will learn much about the merits of marital compromise someday.

"Why do you always pick yellow, Caleb?" I ask.

"Because 'Y' is only two away from 'A'," he explains, making very little sense.

"What do you mean, Caleb?" I pursue.

"Like, instead of A, B, C, you go the other way. A, Z, Y. See?" He says each letter slowly, hoping his grandma will grasp the full meaning of doing the alphabet backward, even when you start with A. I begin mentally moving my linear alphabet into a circular one. "Z comes next to Y, only two away from A," he explains. Then he states his final reasoning: "And yellow begins with Y."

He looks at me over the smears of wet paint, hoping I get the picture. He wants a favorite color that is centered, close to the beginning and close to the end, a yellow flag waving in the circle of infinity. His circumlocution makes me smile.

I hope his wife understands.

Jesus, we admit how incomplete our understanding of you is. You are the Alpha and Omega, the A to Z, the beginning and the end, the infinite Lord of the universe. You encompass every letter of every alphabet; you are the Word made flesh. Help us find our center in the Y word: you. Amen.

32

REMINDERS

Jesus . . . took bread. Having given thanks, he broke it and said, "This is my body, broken for you. Do this to remember me." After supper, he did the same thing with the cup: . . . "Each time you drink this cup, remember me. . . . You will be drawn back to this meal again and again until the Master returns."

1 Corinthians 11:23-26

The words *remembrance* and *remnants* play tag with each other in my thoughts after a family gathering in our home. I smile as I pick up the remnants from the night before (even though parents had done their pass-through pickup as they collected their children). I find ribbons and wrappings, cake crumbs and chocolate syrup smears, handprints on windows and wadded, forgotten diapers in corners. I remember how God left us remnants too: of bread and wine and gospel. What is left most certainly counts. Perhaps it is even holy.

I continue my room-to-room rounds. I choose to believe that picking up remnants is a joyful business. I find a child-sized shoe in the garage, the Johnny Jump Up swing still clinging to a door frame in the family room, stray beads and marbles and Lego pieces on ledges and stairways, in the houseplants, and under furniture. I investigate the toaster as it wafts acrid smoke into the kitchen and find a blue plastic blob clinging to the wire bread-carriage inside. *Oh, no!* I think. *One of the grandkids dropped Grover into the toaster slot. Bold-blue Grover of Sesame Street fame meeting his demise at the hands of an adoring small fry who only wanted to find him a warm home. Oh, dear.* I alert my husband, and together we rescue the blue remains from the crematorium.

On other morning-afters, I discover felt-pen squiggles adorning the peeled firewood next to our wood burning stove. I look at the wall; nothing written there this time. I find our lost cell phone behind couch pillows made into a fort, a stuffed Pooh Bear stuck headfirst in the van window, rice cereal stains mixed with blueberries on my satin blouse, Cheerios doing crunches, and a rosebush looking slightly limp after being doused in outdoor peeing competitions.

One night, in a half doze, I wondered why my husband's hand kept ending up under my back. The next morning as I made the bed, I found Josiah's stuffed friends Camel and Ernie between the bed sheets on my side.

Ah, the remnants that help us remember that love is present in this place.

At last night's party, we celebrated Keith, our oldest son, as he turned thirty-seven and Josiah, son of our youngest son, as he turned three. We sang birthday songs and gave presents. "Do this in remembrance of Me," echoes through the game of tag in my mind as I finish picking up the remnants of our supping and celebrating together. Bread and wine run together in my memory, along with cake crumbs and stuffed camels and Lego pieces.

"Do this!"—until he comes again!

Creative, connecting God, thank you for bread and wine to taste and see and touch that remind us of bigger realities. Thank you that out of a messy crucifixion, a glorious resurrection comes. Thank you that in a messy house, remnants of love abide. Amen.

33

WATCHING

I pray to GOD —my life a prayer—and wait for what
he'll say and do.
My life's on the line before God, my Lord, waiting
and watching till morning. . . .
O Israel, wait and watch for GOD —with GOD's
arrival comes love,
with GOD's arrival comes generous redemption.

Psalm 130:5-7

Lily Kate's eyes were wide open when she came headfirst out of the birth canal. "A rarity," the midwife said in tones of awe. Ever since, Lily Kate watches the world with a wide-eyed gaze that stares and studies, then looks stunned by the surprises she sees.

From her perch in adult arms, Lily observes the slow rhythm of lapping waves, the smoke rising from the barbecue, a fly crawling on the cabin porch, or the antics of brother and cousins playing at her feet. She studies older cousin Anthony's face and then reaches out with her chubby hand to caress his cheeks and nose before discovering that his lips are grab-able. "Look out for Lily," Anthony warns his other boy cousins. "She likes lips!"

When our grandchildren started to talk, they added another dimension to watching: They wanted to be the watched ones. Little Josiah takes a grandpa in one hand and a grandma in the other. "Let's watch *me!*" he says. He drags us out to the trampoline, where he pirouettes in a dizzy dance and asks, "Did you see my fancy feet?" And then, "Watch my octopus," as he jumps and flails all his limbs in different directions.

"Watch me, Grandpa," is the standard invitation for soccer games and saxophone practice, swimming lessons and jumping off stair landings. "Come and watch us, Grandma," becomes the entry into a performance of pedal cars bungee-corded together on the tennis court, a down-home imitation of bumper cars at a carnival. We watch adventure after adventure unfold before our hearts, and we are grateful.

Emmett's parents recite "Jabberwocky" together as he gyrates and falls and slithers to "'Twas brillig, and the slithy toves did gyre and gimble in the wabe."[18] He watches us as we watch him, and then he bows at our applause.

"I think you will be amazed when you see this, Grandma," Sam says to me. I watch as his yo-yo travels up and down on a string. I feel the fifty-five-year-old phantom tugs of a weighted string on my middle finger, moving to a hard-learned rhythm. I am seven again.

Caleb and his mother ask me to come on his second-grade field trip to watch a play at the Children's Theatre. I consent to carpooling my grandson and four of his classmates. After the performance, we meander over to the Seattle Center's fountain to eat our lunch on the benches around the rim. We watch water explode skyward, colorful sunlit geysers programmed to dramatic Bach and Beethoven chords. Every symphonic splash showers hundreds of scavenging pigeons and scatters laughing children. Classmate Chessa shouts to Caleb above the noise, "There's a dove! See it?"

I watch as the singular bird swoops amongst and above mottled gray pigeons and groups of children, pure whiteness fluttering between earth and sky. *How good of God,* my soul sings, *to let me be a part of all this: a grandson's life, a daughter's embrace, the beauty of culture and art, creation and light. It doesn't get any better than this.*

Just watch me; there's more, I hear as God-thoughts enter my epiphany. *I will keep showing up in all your children's and grandchildren's lives. Scattered and diverse though they be, my Spirit will hover, protect, and gather them in. Just sit on the bleachers and watch.*

Watchful God, thank you for being ever-present in our lives. Thank you for the promise that you will never leave us. Put us on daily watch so we do not miss you when you show up. Amen.

34
ENERGY

Be energetic in your life of salvation, reverent and sensitive before God. That energy is God's energy, an energy deep within you, God himself willing and working at what will give him the most pleasure.

Philippians 2:13

Our six-year-old grandson lives with a zest that makes me believe he is the incarnation of "Wow!" In family pictures, some part of Caleb is always blurry. If his grandpa suggests a backyard game of baseball, he shouts, "Batter!" so quickly that everyone else is relegated to fielding. If I want to go for a walk, he races for his helmet and scooter. He loves the trampoline because it defines enthusiasm: jumping up and down with surround-sound laughter. If I tell him what we are having for dinner, he squeals gleefully, "Hurray! That's my favorite!"

He's also passionate about writing and illustrating books, as long as they include families and action and laughter. He has recently self-published *Bunees WiFamles*, a story about bunnies eating humongous carrots with all their rabbit relatives, hopping and smiling broadly because they are feasting together.

Because Caleb likes writing books, his mother buys an empty book for his birthday. She tucks two of his drawings into it. The first is the title page for his book about bunnies; the second is an illustration of Caleb's own family of four: Dad, Mom, big brother, and his own grinning self-portrait.

She puts the empty book on the dining room table and asks the close kin at his party to write a short note in it for him and for memory's sake. Carefully printing large letters, I write, "To Caleb Joseph Francis, who is very special! Thank you for being funny. Thank you for your lively eyes. I like your squeeze-y hugs. Playing baseball with you is so much fun." By this time, Caleb has sidled up to me and is slowly reading out loud what I have written so far. He isn't quite satisfied.

"Grandma, put that I am also fast," he requests. I comply by writing one last sentence: "Caleb is also very fast."

"And put one of those things after it," he says while pointing to the exclamation point at the beginning of the note, right after the word *special*. I add it boldly. He grins. "That's good, Grandma!"

Living life with an exclamation mark. That's our Caleb!

Energizing God, I confess not always feeling exuberant as I grow older. Thank you for the contagious enthusiasm of our grandchildren. I too want to give you pleasure and praise. Help me not to forget the exclamation marks. Amen.

35
WHO AM I?

Your eye is a lamp. . . . If you live wide-eyed in wonder and belief, your body
fills up with light. If you live squinty-eyed
in greed and distrust, your body is a dank cellar. . . . Keep
your life as well-lighted as your best-lighted room.

Luke 11:34-35

I agree to tag along on the semi-annual surfing trip to the Oregon coast. My children make marketing-strategy promises: "You'll have a great time, Mom, sitting on the beach with a book while your grandkids play in the sand around you." My friends incredulously ask, "You're going *where?*" "On a surf trip," I say, as I feel the aura of "with-it Grandma" float down on me like a prophetic mantle.

We take the six-hour trip in my van, loaded with food, clothing, and the thousand items that fall between wet suits and Johnny Jump Ups. I wedge myself into the middle seat between pacifier duty with five-month-old Malakai and toy-trading activities with two-year-old Josiah.

We stop often to do energy-release walk-arounds, to buy a few groceries, to breast-feed the baby, to fill the gas tank, to check out a rest stop for the potty trained, to order tacos at a drive-through. Finally, we reach our destination: an on-site rental trailer at a membership campground near Seaside, Oregon. The van empties; the trailer fills. "I like my little house," Josiah comments. We all need sleep. I volunteer for the bottom bunk.

The next morning at six o'clock I feel a small face next to mine. I open my eyes to see an Eeyore expression full of patient sadness on my little grandson that turns immediately into a "She's alive!" ecstasy. The day begins.

Later that morning we hike the quarter mile to where the surf is up. I strap a folding beach chair on one shoulder, a diaper bag on the other, balance a shovel between the two, hang on to my book bag with one free hand, and hold Josiah's hand with the other to keep him from falling off the path into a ravine. I self-talk: "You can make it." "What great exercise!" "Don't think about having to do this all over again tomorrow." "You can rest when you get to the beach."

We meet our group of seventy-five other surfers and surfer supporters when we reach the hallowed spot where the waves come in. I set up my beach chair. Before I can settle, some sensitive soul moves it inland because I am in tide's way. Another offers a fold-a-tent for my grandbaby. I watch my children get into their wet suits, a claustrophobic activity akin to being stuck in an MRI tube for an afternoon. They eagerly grab surfboards and go out to sea.

After several hours, I feel a stuck-ness too, but not because I am immobile. My four grandchildren do not simply play at my feet. I walk the baby to sleep, bury children in the sand, rescue them from incoming waves, respond to their "Watch this!" I realize that to those in this surfing company, I am "just the grandmother."

Others have no knowledge of my history, my professional life, my struggles, or my victories. I begin to ask with Bonhoeffer, "Who am I?" I do not read a single page from a book; I do not sit except with a sleeping baby in my arms.

My eyes take in the beach's beauty, the waves' relentless faithfulness, the shimmering sunlight, and my grandbaby's face. As sea breeze caresses my face, I have an epiphany: This is the day I am a grandmother; I do rejoice and am glad in it!

We go back to the trailer, our little house. Josiah discovers the magnetic-latched door under the table's bench. He throws his miniature toy truck and driver into the cavity, followed by a stuffed bunny. Then he goes into the cavern for the rescue. "Shut the door, Grandma," I hear in hollow tones. He stays in there while I remain poised for possible little-boy panic or "Open the door" orders. I sip my coffee. Suddenly the door bursts open; Josiah crawls out and wriggles his little frame into an upright position. His eyes get used to the light. I see pure joy written on his face.

"I found me!" he shouts. The darkness is gone; discovery has come.

Lord, we echo the prayer of Dietrich Bonhoeffer: "Who am I? They mock me, these lonely questions of mine. Whoever I am, thou knowest, O God, I am thine."[19] *Amen.*

PART SIX

CHILDLIKE FAITH

The disciples came to Jesus asking, "Who gets the highest rank in God's kingdom?" For an answer Jesus called over a child, whom he stood in the middle of the room, and said, "I'm telling you, once and for all, that unless you return to square one and start over like children, you're not even going to get a look at the kingdom, let alone get in. Whoever becomes simple and elemental again, like this child, will rank high in God's kingdom. What's more, when you receive the childlike on my account, it's the same as receiving me."

Matthew 18:1-5

36
THE CROSS

*For my part, I am going to boast about nothing but
the Cross of our Master, Jesus Christ.*

Galatians 6:14

I come through the screen door carrying napkins and utensils just in time to hear the click of plastic. I see two grandsons seated on the picnic bench, knocking their sippy cups together and shouting, "Cheers!" I smile at their joyful ritual in response to summer sunshine and visiting cousins, then begin wondering where in the world they picked *that* up.

I notice this theme carried further. "Let's do nose cheers, Mommy," one of them says and then initiates a nose rub with his cooperating mother. Later, while the two cousins are sipping root beer, I hear, "Let's do straw cheers." I watch them take dripping straws from their drinks and touch them like crossed swords. "Cheers!" they exclaim in unison.

If children were to sign on with an affinity group, it would be called Monkey See, Monkey Do. Repeated images catch their attention. Repeated actions charm them into imitation.

Three-year-old Josiah stands on the high-backed ridge of our love seat in order to touch and caress the embossed designs on an old medieval cross hanging there. Later we take him with us to visit relatives who have just lost a teenage granddaughter in an accident. Sorrow and silence commingle in the heavy summer air. As words elude us, we welcome the distraction of watching our grandson scoot a toy truck across the patio floor, then wander between potted flowers on the deck's perimeter. He stops at a scraggly plant and addresses the makeshift trellis—a thin, vertical stick stapled to a horizontal one—stuck in the dry dirt. "Hi, cross," he says and then moves on. A reminder of Jesus. We are comforted.

A friend's grandchild, attending a Catholic school for the first time, becomes aware of the crucifixes in the hallways and classrooms. She comes home and, to the "How's school?" question, says, "Jesus likes math a lot." "Why do you say that?" her parents query. "Because he's always on a plus sign," she answers.

On Easter morning, Anthony asks a myriad of questions about how Jesus died on the cross. His dad explains the painful agony of trying to take a breath when limbs are pierced and lungs collapsed. "Was it like this, Dad?" Anthony asks as he stands up away from the table, putting his arms out as if hanging on a cross and his feet together as if impaled to a board. Straining, he pushes up onto his tiptoes, sticks out his chest, pretends struggle as he lifts his head, and takes gulps of breath. I suck in mine as I watch our eight-year-old grandson doing his best to imitate Christ.

Josiah comes home from his three-year-olds Sunday school class wearing a construction paper cross on a string of purple yarn. He notices it still hanging around his neck when his mother removes his jacket. His eyes dart to the gold cross on a chain around her neck. "Let's do cross cheers," he suggests as he lifts his cross to hers and touches it lightly. "Cheers!" he says.

Thank you, Master God, for preordaining a salvation symbol so simple that a child can readily recognize it. You knew their little eyes would be drawn to where the crossbeams cross, focusing in on the face of Jesus. We acknowledge and boast in the cross of Jesus. Cheers! and Amen!

37

DREAMS AND IMAGINATION

*God can do anything, you know—far more than you could ever imagine or
guess or request in your wildest dreams! He does it not by pushing us around
but by working within us, his Spirit
deeply and gently within us.*

Ephesians 3:20

I drop by just as Sam and Jack's mother comes out of their bedroom. They have said their prayers and quieted down for the evening after their first day of school in second grade and kindergarten. She assures me that I won't break any rhythms or rituals if I surprise them with yet another "Good night."

I belt out a 1950s Sinatra song as I waltz into their room: "Good night, Irene. Good night, Irene. I'll see you in my dreams." Sinatra would cringe at my solo techniques; my grandchildren giggle at my gusto. I hope loving spontaneity is a form of Christlike craziness.

"That's a song Grandpa and I sang when we were young," I say as I tuck Jack's covers under his neck. "I think I would like to see *you* in my dreams tonight, Jack. Where would you like to be, and what would you like to be doing?"

"Just put me with people we know, like Mom and Dad, and Grandpa and you, and Sam. And make the backgrounds your house or your outside—the real things, not the imaginary ones," Jack says. Then he counsels, "Just don't imagine things. Sometimes imaginary things get mad at you in dreams. Like a sofa that comes to life because you're thinking too hard. Not really to eat you—it just wants to scare you."

"What do you do when you have a scary dream, Jack?" I ask, knowing that his parents have talked to him before about his nightmares, suggesting ways to turn his fears into more pleasant fantasies.

"If there was a monster or a dinosaur, I could probably throw him a fresh piece of meat, especially if it was a T. rex." He pauses as creative thoughts continue to nudge and jostle somewhere between his head and his heart fears. "And I haven't done this, but it would be fun: Just say hello and maybe they would say hello back and wave at me." Jack's imagination cannot be quieted.

"And if Sam is in your dream, no bees and no red ants, because he'll scream and wake you up."

On cue, Sam enters the dialogue, bedded down after one day of second-grade status. "Know where I want to be in your dream? I want to be sitting at a desk, in a schoolroom, with a pencil, doing math."

"And using your brain, right?" I add.

"Yeah," Sam agrees. "Put that in your dream, Grandma."

I recall for them some dream input from a younger grandson who lives fifty miles up the road: "When your cousin Emmett was traveling home the other night, he was looking out the car window and saw a star shining through the clouds. What do you think he said?"

Sam and Jack listen in anticipatory silence.

"He said, 'There's a star in heaven. Maybe it's a kid, flying in his dreams, and he has a flashlight.'"

I leave them with two quick good-night kisses and their imaginations.

Jack's last thought trails after me: "Grandma, I have this little guy with a beard and he's a hundred years old. When I want him to, he takes me back from my dreams."

"I'm glad, Jack," I say.

As I close their bedroom door, I wonder who or what will show up in each of our dreams during the night as we sleep. I imagine that, because of the dark, the Holy Spirit will be carrying the light to show us the way home.

God, whose image we hold within us, thank you for dreams while we sleep and daydreams while awake. May the Holy Spirit work gently and deeply within our grandchildren's worst nightmares and fondest dreams. Lead each of us, we pray, through every dark night that threatens our souls and every bright vision that lights up your purposes. Amen.

38

GROWTH

No prolonged infancies among us, please. . . . God wants us to grow up, to know the whole truth and tell it in love—like Christ in everything. . . . He keeps us in step with each other.

Ephesians 4:14-16

Four-year-old Emmett measures growth. After we coax him to eat his eggs at a family breakfast picnic ("They'll help you grow, Emmett!"), he jumps off the edge of the patio and then scoots in front of his cousin Jack, their protruding tummies bouncing off each other like soft beach balls. Emmett pokes Jack's stomach and announces, "It's grown!" Then he offers his tummy to Jack for palpation. "Did I grow, Jack?" Next he stands back-to-back with older cousin Sam for a height check.

"How tall do you think Sam is, Emmett?" I ask.

"One foot, three inches," he answers authoritatively.

I wonder if experts on the birth order of siblings have done any studies on cousins. Perhaps Emmett focuses on "growing" because he is the fifth-born cousin, following a six-year-old, two sevens, and an eight. He proudly wears his hand-me-down Batman underwear from older cousin Jack. He gets a USA flag T-shirt from Sam and insists on wearing it four days in a row, even though he's Canadian. Bigger cousins' clothes no doubt add to one's stature.

We watch a robin at its morning feeding. "Look, Grandma," Emmett says. "He sticks out his tongue every time he hops." We talk about how the robin is finding bugs and worms on our big green plate of lawn so that it can grow. "And maybe even tiny frogs," he adds. *Big* and *tiny*: his well-used vocabulary words. A large horsefly buzzes around our shoulders, and Emmett tells me it's the same one that was in their car when they arrived earlier. That afternoon we observe a tiny fly dizzy-buzzing against a window inside the cabin. "Is that the same fly, Emmett?" I ask. Emmett pauses and studies the insect, then shakes his head. "This one's name is Junior," he says.

Not only does he want to be like his older cousins in size, he wants to do what they can do. When Grandpa rides his four-wheeler and lets the older boys take turns manning the controls, Emmett, who cannot quite reach the steering wheel, is consigned to the "holding box" behind Grandpa with two-year-old Josiah. He slumps in his seat, wishing, I suspect, for arms an inch or two longer. "I like the feer-whooler!" Josiah says enthusiastically, trying to cheer his older cousin.

Emmett's father generates a commando game in the woods for the older children. They hide behind trees, run for cover behind bushes, and pretend to talk on their walkie-talkies while heading for home base. Emmett has a hard time keeping up; deflated, he lags and then cries. In an effort to comfort him and lay out a solution, his parents encourage him to practice his running. They find a stopwatch and tell Emmett that they will time him as he runs around the cabin. He is motivated. His upper body lunges forward at "Go!" His little legs lope clumsily to keep up. Red-faced after the last corner turn, he comes in for a speed check. "One minute and ten seconds," his mom says. Before his dad can explain "personal best," Emmett takes off running again. "You went faster than last time, Emmett," his mom says, clicking the stopwatch. He runs around the cabin again and again. We applaud his persistence.

When his mother was pregnant with his little sister, Emmett began tummy measuring at the six-month mark by wrapping his small arms around his mother's middle and commenting often, "It is taking a very long time for our baby to be ready." Sometime during the ninth month, Emmett, whose height positions him perfectly, planted a spontaneous kiss on his mother's protruding belly and then said loudly, in order to reach the tiny someone through womb walls, "Hello, baby, I'm your *big* brother."

Father, we know you want us to grow up and grow toward you. We thank you for being in charge of every growth and spurt of our development, physically and spiritually, mentally and emotionally. Measure us not against your perfection, Father; measure us, we plead, according to your mercy. Amen.

39

BRICKS AND BUBBLES

"I came so they can have real and eternal life, more and better life than they ever dreamed of."

John 10:10

The remodeling projects continue at our daughter's home in Seattle. Today we look forward to doing demolition and dump runs. We hook our empty farm trailer to our vehicle and make the hour-long trek into the city.

Our grandsons' greeting is full of party mood: "Let's play! Grandpa and Grandma are here!" Their parents do the motivational twisting: "First we have to work. When we get all the old chimney bricks from the upstairs into Grandpa's trailer, you can go along to the dump and get a milkshake on the way."

Grandpa is assigned to tying and loading bags of old insulation. Their father takes a crowbar to the upstairs bathroom, removing fiberglass and dismantling toilet and tub. Their mother uses the electric drill to take off old hardware from salvageable doors and cupboards. Grandma and the boys examine the pile of bricks.

"How many trips downstairs to the trailer is this going to take?" I ask. Together we calculate. "If Anthony and Caleb can each carry one brick per trip and Grandma can carry two . . ."

"About twenty trips each," we estimate.

Our first round of eager energy kicks in, despite summer heat. The hot air in the gutted upstairs is laden with insulation particles and brick dust and ninety-year-old decay. We languish under our Egyptian-slave burdens. Their mother re-motivates: "Ten more trips each, and you can have a Popsicle." I try to be a good example of a hard worker in spite of screaming hips (is that arthritis or osteoporosis?) and raw arms where the gloves fail to provide cover. I pass each boy on the stairwell, faking smiles and a cheer that announces the trip number we are on. "That's seventeen. Here goes eighteen." The bricks get heavier.

As the pile disappears, we notice an even larger pile of bricks hidden behind the studs. Our shoulders and our spirits droop. At least we made it to Popsicle time. Sitting at the patio table, sucking our berry flavors in the sunshine, we regroup. The three of us brainstorm a plan for unexpected pile number two: If Jesus were here, he could order a tornado to touch down on that brick pile and just carry it away. Winds and waves listen to him, after all.

Their father is our next choice. We commandeer him to sit upstairs beside the brick pile and hand a brick to me. Then I hand it in turn to Anthony, then on to Caleb standing on a plywood island over floor joists, who passes it to Grandpa sitting in the open window. Grandpa gives the brick a fling into the trailer below, missing the roof and rain gutter with a hook shot reminiscent of his basketball days. No more up and down the stairs. Our brick brigade works. We get into a rhythm. Together we sing, "I've been working on the railroad, all the livelong day. . . ."[20] Brick pile number two disappears into dump-run oblivion. We claim victory by relaxing on the back patio once again.

Tired boys don't stop all activity, however. They haul a gallon of bubble-blowing liquid next to my chair and hand me the plastic bubble maker. "Blow us some bubbles, Grandma!" My tired arms and lungs rejuvenate. Work done, I enter play. Weightless bubbles after heavy bricks sound manageable. The children grab sticks and broom handles and fly swatters. They laugh and pop and catch and chase. A light breeze carries the bubbles off to the right, then the left. Sometimes the bubbles lift straight up into the sky. The wind puffs make the bubble game much more fun.

The breezes continue, fickle. Anthony stops his flailing and tries to figure out why. He sits, watching the bubbles swirl, and then quietly says, "I think a tornado's starting, Grandma."

You are Lord over bricks and bubbles, over work and play, over the heavy and the light, over the winds and the waves. We live safely — abundantly! — all because of you. Amen.

40
DRAGONFLIES

Light, space, zest—that's GOD!
So, with him on my side I'm fearless, afraid of no one
and nothing.

Psalm 27:1

Emmett, who is two and a half, lives with his parents near downtown Vancouver, BC, in an apartment complex. He does short spurts of summering with us at our backwoods cabin in Montana. He also does short sentences, for the first time putting words to his wilderness experiences. After several days of seeing no cars and no city folks, he announces, slowly, like a bell going ding-dong twice, "There's-no traf-fic!"

He seems nearly fearless as he faces the outdoor adventures his grandfather and I offer him. He skinny-dips in our mountain creek and learns a new meaning for "Cold!" He falls out of a canoe into the lake. A life jacket and his adrenaline-saturated father save him. He calmly says, "That was funny."

He and I take his miniature red Matchbox bulldozer down the lane one afternoon and use it to move the layers of pine needles carpeting a half mile of driveway. Unafraid of the acres and acres of forest on every side inhabited by he knows not what, he bulldozes mounds of lightweight needles into roads and bridges and hills and valleys, setting up a small kingdom in the state of Montana. "I like it," he says when he finishes.

The only thing that puts fear in his eyes and sets him to running are the dragonflies. Grown large as two crossed Popsicle sticks, they whir like little helicopters. They fly close to Emmett's ears, and his little arms flail around his head to ward them off. "Help!" he cries, and one of us who loves him catches up with him, enfolds him, and protectively shields him from this perceived threat. We explain to him that dragonflies are beautiful, blue, and shimmery and that they won't hurt him. He tries to be braver the next time the dragonflies zoom.

A few weeks have passed, and I am in San Francisco looking through art galleries with my daughter. We find some original Picassos. We learn that at one point in his career, Picasso was asked to illustrate a textbook on animals and insects. There it was, straight from the book, framed and hanging, a six-by-eight-inch original ink drawing of a dragonfly. Next to the picture, the gallery's director had placed a telling quote: "Art is all about putting your fears on paper."

I wish I had an extra four thousand dollars. I would give the Picasso to Emmett to hang in his room—a reminder to live fearlessly, even with a dragonfly close by.

Lord, thank you that whether we find ourselves in Vancouver or Montana or San Francisco wildernesses, you are there. Thank you that we have nothing to fear in all of creation because of your care. Amen.

41

HASSLES

*The disciples came to Jesus asking, "Who gets the highest rank
in God's kingdom?"
For an answer Jesus called over a child, whom he stood in
the middle of the room, and said, ". . . Whoever becomes simple and elemental
again, like this child, will rank high in God's kingdom. What's more, when
you receive the childlike on my account, it's the same as receiving me."*

Matthew 18:1-5

Whoever thought up the word *hassle* must have just finished putting small children to bed—or just served on a second-century creed
committee trying to decide between heresy and truth.

To get Caleb undressed and pajama-ed, I use every persuasive
word in my warm-and-loving-grandmother phrase book. "Wow,
Caleb, you get to wear your dinosaur jammies tonight." "Right after
you brush your teeth, you can have your yummy purple vitamin."
"Let's find your blankie and Corsilie [his name for a ratty stuffed ter-
rier], and then we'll read a story."

Caleb has "fitting" issues. (Maybe the church does too, now
that I think of it.) When the heel of his sock doesn't hug his own
heel with perfect snugness, he tries another pair. If the elastic on his
pajama bottoms pinches his abdomen at a touchy nerve ending, off
they come. If the sleeves on his pajama tops get too cozy with his
arms, they are history. So he often sleeps in his underwear.

Conversely, his older brother, Anthony, is a speed-dresser. He
throws his pajamas over his stick-skinny limbs so quickly, I don't
know whether he still has his day clothes (or his underwear, for that
matter) underneath them. And what are the current rules their parents want enforced? Pajamas or not? Underwear off or on?

These simple quandaries pale in the light of the doctrinal discussion that follows. Caleb climbs to the top bunk and Anthony burrows into the lower one, as usual. Tradition claims them, even at age six and seven. Bedtime prayers are next.

"So, what can we thank God for tonight?" I ask. There is silence. The stall techniques have started.

"How about thanking God for colors?" I suggest. We had opened brand-new poster paints just before bedtime, and the boys had savored the dipping and mixing and painting.

"Not that, Grandma," Caleb answers. "Everything is really germs. The paints are germs; even my blanket." I try to track his prayer theology: *We probably do not thank God for bad things like germs, but his beloved blanket? Not if it, too, is germ-laden.*

"Except us," Anthony enters the dialogue. "We're not germs; we're mud."

Caleb gets wide-eyed with understanding. He is seated cross-legged, dead center on the top bunk in a pontifical position. He states his brother's insight like a dictum from the Vatican: "Grandma, we are just dried mud!"

Anthony continues, "Every time Jesus finds some mud, he makes a baby. But you don't get to be a person until Sunday." I try to fill in the gaps between the Genesis account of the creation of man, Jesus' redemption of humankind, the origin of personhood, and attending church. I cannot. I begin to wonder how to untangle what clearly makes sense to my grandsons.

So I ask, "What happens on Sunday, Anthony?"

"You get baptized into the family. That's when you're a person," he explains.

I process these simple truths: belief, baptism, and belonging. Theologians of the ages, step aside. The hassles are over; the profound has come. Listen to the child in the middle of the room.

Lord of little ones, thank you for our children and grandchildren who call us back to simple and elemental faith in you. Amen.

42

*But whoever did want him, who believed he was who he claimed and would
do what he said, He made to be their true selves, their child-of-God selves.*

John 1:12

Preschooler Jack presents his grandpa and me with his latest master-
piece for the refrigerator door: a penciled depiction of pointy-moun-
tain terrain crawling with stick warriors fighting the bad guys down
in a gully. Our pictorial prophet draws on a universal theme once
again: good versus evil.

I imagine *Life* magazine wanting Jack's early childhood drawings
when he becomes famous someday, so I ask him to sit down and
write his signature on his latest art rendering. He cooperates by picking up the pencil, leaning heavily over his paper, and making a slow,
deliberate curve down and to the right to form the letter J. The end
of the curve goes off the right-hand edge of the page. Victoriously
he caps the backward letter with a short horizontal line. There is no
room left for the rest of his name.

"My teacher and mom are helping me with my letters," he
informs me, "so I don't do them backward anymore."

Next he moves his pencil to the left of the J and makes two
slanted lines to form the pyramid shape of the A.

"How am I doin', Grandma?" he asks as he puts his horizontal
victory line into the middle of the A. He starts on the C.

I waffle. Do I tell him, along with his two other mentors, that he
is still making his letters backward? Does he really need three teachers niggling him? Can grandmas lie out of loving care and still keep
their moral integrity?

I notice that the A is not backward.

"You're doing just fine, Jack," I encourage. He signs off with a backward C and K, "mirror writing" at its finest.

I worry enough to do some research. Left-handed fifteenth-century artist Leonardo da Vinci mirror-wrote his personal notes. Historians suppose that either he didn't want people to steal his ideas; or he was hiding his scientific observations from the church, whose teachings sometimes disagreed with his; or he simply didn't want to smudge his wet ink. Hebrew is also written from right to left. Jack is in good company.

I wonder how many letters in the alphabet are not reversible, how many letters Jack will automatically "get right." I write them down and discover he can be correct almost half the time—not enough, but a good start. After the A, the next three letters are H, I, M, followed by O, T, U, V, W, X, and Y. My eyes fix on the only word within the eleven-letter string: Him. Word association, from memorizing King James verses in my youth, moves my mind to "In all thy ways acknowledge him, and he shall direct thy paths" (Proverbs 3:6). My trust level grows. The God of great reversals can turn anything around: The last shall be first, the blind see, the lame walk, the lost found, the dying live.

Lives can turn around. So can alphabet letters. A child can help an adult grow, even if the adult has a waffling conscience or questioning mind.

"You're doing just fine, Jack."

God of reversals, change us and set us on a straight path. God of change, transform us into our "child-of-God selves." From generation to generation, we trust you and thank you. Amen.

CONCLUSION

Our ninth grandchild, Isabel Malia, burst into our lives on a September day months after the stories of our eight grandchildren were already in the editing room at NavPress. Orv and I had thought we were finished welcoming grandbabies. We rejoiced at not being done yet.

My book is not really finished either, I am told; it needs a conclusion page. The morning of my writing deadline, Isabel's mother told my husband and me a story of taking her three little ones to the park. As we sat in the kitchen booth listening, the table, covered with toys and food, served as our campfire pit. Happy camper Isabel leaned into her high-chair tray as she smeared and blobbed her pretty baby face with a saliva-soaked teething cookie. Two-year-old Malakai toddled around the table, a soaked diaper weighing him down — two parts lake water and three parts his own doing. First words, first sentences, came out of the sides of his mouth as they made their way around his pacifier. "Fixth da guy, Gramma," he requested as he handed me a Playmobile figure whose hands are engineered to click on to a miniature bicycle's handlebars. Four-year-old Josiah smiled as he ate his peanut butter sandwich and remembered his snack request: a lion sandwich. His mother had handed him a piece of brown bread folded over a plastic toy lion; they owned a joke together.

We adults settled into attentiveness amid the distractions.

"After we had been at the park awhile, the boys noticed the lake," our daughter-in-law said. "I'm trying to let go a little, trying not to be such a control freak . . . let my kids make messes. So when Josiah asked if he could put his cloth Grinch in the lake at the park and give him a bath, I said okay. But then Malakai tried copying his brother, only he chucked his stuffed toy three feet out into the lake."

The group around the campfire listened and grinned.

"So I laid Isabel on a blanket and told Josiah to sit by her and put his hand on her back so she wouldn't roll down the hill. Then I waded in to rescue the drowning toy. That explains my wet sweatpants."

Still multitasking, she turned to the messy baby gnawing her cookie and began teaching her the sign language she had taught earlier to Isabel's big brothers. *Are we ever done parenting?* I think with tired joy.

"More?" this mommy asked as she brought the tips of all her fingers together in a back-and-forth motion. "Or are you all-l-l-l done?" she sang, twisting both hands upward several times.

Good questions for any unfinished meal or day or life. As long as we breathe, we will clean up messes, keep each other from rolling downhill, pull off rescues, tell the stories, and find awe and wonder.

I have learned to keep expecting more stories from the eternal God who dreamed up the Resurrection. Love and truth irrepressibly erupt when children are present—the truth that Jesus lives in us, that he is the Author of our stories and the Finisher of our faith, and that he joins us around the campfire.

Notes

1. Eugene Peterson, *Living the Resurrection: The Risen Christ in Everyday Life* (Colorado Springs, CO: NavPress, 2006), 53, 58.

2. Gina Bria, "A Book of Hours," *Mars Hill Review*, Number 15/Fall 1999, 10.

3. Aesop, "The Fox and the Crow," *Aesop's Fables*, paraphrase of translation from www.AesopFables.com.

4. In some cities, it also signals that there are drugs for sale in the area.

5. Dr. Seuss, *Dr. Seuss's ABC* (New York: Random House, 1963, 1991), 3–5.

6. Seuss, 16.

7. Seuss, 63.

8. C. S. Lewis, *The Four Loves* (New York: Harcourt, 1960), 126, 92. Copyright © 1960 by Helen Joy Lewis and renewed 1988 by Arthur Owen Barfield. Reprinted by permission of Harcourt, Inc.

9. Paul Fleischman, *Weslandia* (Cambridge, MA: Candlewick, 1999), 7.

10. "Hark! the Herald Angels Sing," National Union of Christian Schools, ed., *Let Youth Praise Him! A Hymnal for Christian Primary Schools, Sunday Schools and Christian Homes* (Grand Rapids, MI: Eerdmans, 1952), 75. Words: Charles Wesley, 1739. Music: Felix Mendelssohn, 1840.

11. Monique Duval, *The Persistence of Yellow: A Book of Recipes for Life* (Edmonds, WA: Compendium, 2000), 204.

12. Effie Crockett, "Rock-a-Bye, Baby," 1872, http://en.wikipedia.org/wiki/Rock-a-bye_Baby.

13. David Rutherford McGuire and William B. Bradbury, "Jesus Loves Me," 1862, http://www.cyberhymnal.org/htm/j/e/jesuslme.htm.

14. Henri J. M. Nouwen, *Life of the Beloved: Spiritual Living in a Secular World* (New York: Crossroad, 2000), 48–49.

15. Mabel Watts, *The Story of Zachary Zween* (New York: Parents' Magazine, 1967), 1–2, 4.

16. Eugene Peterson, "Introduction to Malachi," *The Message Numbered Edition* (Colorado Springs, CO: NavPress, 2002), 1319.

17. J. I. Packer, *C. S. Lewis: The Man from Narnia*, (Vancouver: Regent, 2003), CD.

18. Lewis Carroll, "Jabberwocky," as quoted by Louis Untermeyer in *Doorways to Poetry* (New York: Harcourt, 1938), 132.

19. Dietrich Bonhoeffer, *The Cost of Discipleship* (New York: Collier, 1963), 20.

20. "I've Been Working on the Railroad," http://www.answers.com/topic/i-ve-been-working-on-the-railroad.

About the Author

DONNA VANDER GRIEND is a grandmother who has found a way to ignore the clock by connecting with people, whether young or old, family or stranger. As "networker" at Sonlight Community Church, she encouraged people to grow toward God while "one-anothering" each other through mentoring and small groups.

She served as chaplain/counselor for middle and high school students for a dozen years, trained leaders on friendship evangelism for the Coffee Break Ministry of the Christian Reformed Church throughout the western U.S. and Canada, and has authored four books.

Donna first glimpsed her husband of forty-three years, Orv, shooting baskets in an old gym with other junior high boys; Orv first sighted Donna pitching a softball in a crinoline-poufed skirt and dainty flat shoes. They dated in college, married just before Orv started medical school, had four babies, and survived a life of "on-calls" because of a very gracious God. Nine grandchildren have since added dialogue and plot that begged for this book to be written.

Donna takes joy in "seeing through a glass darkly," noticing the shiny blur of hope in the distance, and pushing through people's flaws and murky situations to find God at work and play.

Contact Donna at donnavdg@earthlink.net or by writing to 5225 E. North Street, Bellingham, WA 98226.

NAVPRESS TITLES TO INSPIRE AND REFRESH YOU.

If You Can't Lose It, Decorate It

Anita Renfroe   1-57683-994-X

It seems that no matter what we try, we're constantly stuck with a part of us we'd rather not have. From weight control to childhood issues to personality quirks, trying to change our situations can be overwhelming. With her contagious spirit, Anita shows us that while some issues are here to stay, attitude makes all the difference between existing and thriving.

The Feminine Soul

Janet Davis   1-57683-817-X

Using biblical stories that highlight women, *The Feminine Soul* illustrates God's true intentions for the women of his kingdom. Author Janet Davis brings spiritual clarity and hope to women so they can recognize and celebrate the intimate love of God for their unique feminine identity.

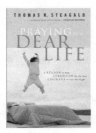

Praying for Dear Life

Thomas R. Steagald   1-57683-816-1

Drawing on decades of pastoral experience, Thomas Steagald crafts an inspiring work filled with lyrical anecdotes, Southern wit, and scriptural reflection.

To get your copies, visit your local Christian bookstore, call NavPress at 1-800-366-7788, or log on to www.navpress.com.

To locate a Christian bookstore near you, call 1-800-991-7747.

NAVPRESS®
BRINGING TRUTH TO LIFE
www.navpress.com